OUTDOOR ADVENTURE AND SOCIAL THEORY

Adventure sports – from rock climbing to freestyle kayaking – are a modern social phenomenon that can tell us much about the relationship between sport, culture and contemporary society. In this engaging new introductory text, adventure sports are used to illustrate key concepts in social theory and to demonstrate why an understanding of social theory is essential for any student taking a course in sport, adventure or outdoor education.

Each chapter in the book introduces a key 'classical' or modern social theorist, such as Marx, Durkheim, Weber or Elias, or a universal topic or issue in social theory, such as sustainability, commodification or identity. Within each of the chapters the theorist or topic is brought to life through case studies of adventurous activities and lived experiences, helping the reader to connect their own sporting and adventurous interests with the frameworks we use to understand wider culture and society. Concise and full of cutting-edge contemporary examples, *Outdoor Adventure and Social Theory* is the perfect companion for any module on the sociology of sport, adventure or outdoor recreation.

Elizabeth C.J. Pike is Head of Sport Development and Management, Reader in the Sociology of Sport and Exercise and Chair of the Anita White Foundation at the University of Chichester, UK. She co-authored *Sports in Society: Issues and Controversies* and is the current President of the International Sociology of Sport Association.

Simon Beames is the programme director of the MSc in Outdoor Ed... at the University of Edinburgh, UK. He is co-author of *Le...* and editor of *Understanding Educational Expeditions*.

'I teach a course in the philosophy of leisure, and I feel like I am fairly knowledgeable about outdoor recreation and social theory. When I read Marx, Weber, and other scholars I knew well, the chapters in this book clarified my thinking. When I dove into theorists less familiar to me (e.g. Foucault, Elias), I immediately discovered new directions my philosophy course needed to take. *Outdoor Adventure and Social Theory* will markedly improve my own teaching.'

Steven Simpson, University Graduate Director and Recreation Management and Therapeutic Recreation Chair, University of Wisconsin-La Crosse, USA

'Aimed at making social theory relevant to, and accessible for under-graduate students on the growing array of outdoor education and adventure courses that are emerging, *Outdoor Adventure and Social Theory* does just that. Written in an engaging and accessible way, it draws together an impressive array of academic experts who are also adventure sports enthusiasts. Its remit is comprehensive and challenging; each chapter showing how a particular theoretical perspective helps to understand these sporting practices. It starts with the seminal thinkers in classic social theory (Karl Marx, Emile Durkheim and Max Weber), then moves through more contemporary thinkers (e.g. Giddens and Foucault). Chapters also focus on important themes in the contemporary adventure landscape, such as the impact of globalisation, and how adventure practices impact negatively on the environment. This book will be a really valuable textbook for undergraduate students across the range of outdoor education courses, and will also appeal to those who participate in, or have interest in, outdoor and adventurous activities.'

Dr Belinda Wheaton, Principal Research Fellow, University of Brighton, UK

OUTDOOR ADVENTURE AND SOCIAL THEORY

Edited by Elizabeth C.J. Pike
and Simon Beames

Routledge
Taylor & Francis Group

LONDON AND NEW YORK

First published 2013
by Routledge
2 Park Square, Milton Park, Abingdon, Oxon OX14 4RN

Simultaneously published in the USA and Canada
by Routledge
711 Third Avenue, New York, NY 10017

Routledge is an imprint of the Taylor & Francis Group, an informa business

British Library Cataloguing in Publication Data
A catalogue record for this book is available from the British Library

Library of Congress Cataloging-in-Publication Data
Outdoor adventure and social theory / edited by Elizabeth Pike and
Simon Beames.
p. cm.
1. Endurance sports. 2. Outdoor recreation. 3. Sports–Sociological aspects.
I. Pike, Elizabeth. II. Beames, Simon.
GV749.5.O88 2013
796.046–dc23
2012043207

ISBN: 978-0-415-53266-2 (hbk)
ISBN: 978-0-415-53267-9 (pbk)
ISBN: 978-0-203-11477-3 (ebk)

Typeset in Bembo
by Keystroke, Station Road, Codsall, Wolverhampton

MIX
Paper from
responsible sources
FSC® C018575
www.fsc.org

Printed and bound in Great Britain by MPG Printgroup

To our students over the years: Thanks for the discussions and debates that have enhanced our own understandings of social theory and its applications. (SKB & ECJP)

CONTENTS

CONTRIBUTORS

Linda Allin is a principal lecturer in the Department of Sport Development at Northumbria University. Her PhD explored 'Women's careers in outdoor education', and she was one of the co-editors of the *Journal of Adventure Education and Outdoor Learning* from 2007 to 2012. Her main outdoor adventures involve kayaking and playing on white water.

Michael Atkinson is associate professor and ethnographer of physical culture in the Faculty of Kinesiology and Physical Education at the University of Toronto. His teaching and research interests focus on movement cultures, bioethics, violence and figurational sociology.

Simon Beames is the programme director of the MSc in Outdoor Education at the University of Edinburgh. He is co-author of *Learning outside the Classroom* (Routledge, 2011) and editor of *Understanding Educational Expeditions* (Sense, 2010).

Paul Beedie is currently head of department (acting), PE and Sport Studies at the University of Bedfordshire. He is an experienced rock climber and mountaineer. His research has been driven by an interest in adventure and includes explorations of risk, identity and community.

Mike Brown is a senior lecturer in the Department of Sport and Leisure Studies at the University of Waikato, New Zealand. His research and teaching focus is outdoor education. His recent work promotes place-responsive approaches to teaching and learning in the outdoors. He is a keen sailor – when time allows.

Carl Cater teaches tourism at Aberystwyth University, Wales, and his research centres on the experiential turn in tourism and the subsequent growth of special interest sectors, particularly adventure tourism and ecotourism. He is a fellow of the Royal Geographical Society, a qualified pilot, diver, lifesaver, mountain and tropical forest leader, and maintains an interest in both the practice and pursuit of sustainable outdoor tourism activity.

Greg Dash is a doctoral student at Aberystwyth University, Wales, studying the effect of wind farm development on tourists and the visitor economy. He has an interest in critical theory and politics.

Chris Loynes has worked in outdoor education as a teacher and youth worker. He founded the profession's journal, *Adventure Education and Outdoor Leadership*, in 1980. Since then he has been teaching, researching and writing about the field as a university lecturer and educational advisor.

Ken McCulloch is a senior lecturer at the University of Edinburgh. His teaching and research interests centre around young people and non-school, non-formal education, including youth work and, particularly, sail training. In his spare time he is a co-owner of an 'almost-classic' yacht.

Elizabeth C.J. Pike is head of Sport Development and Management, reader in the Sociology of Sport and Exercise, and chair of the Anita White Foundation at the University of Chichester. She co-authored *Sports in Society: Issues and Controversies* and is the current President of the International Sociology of Sport Association.

Kate Rawles works half-time as a senior lecturer in Outdoor Studies and half-time as a freelance writer, lecturer and environmental campaigner. Her book *The Carbon Cycle: Crossing the Great Divide* (Two Ravens Press, 2012) uses an adventure bike ride in the Rocky Mountains to explore climate change and was short-listed for the 2012 Banff Mountain Festival book awards (Adventure Travel category). She is a keen sea-kayaker and hill-walker, as well as a cyclist, and lives in the Lake District.

John Telford has worked with groups in the outdoors for fifteen years. He is currently a post-doctoral fellow at Simon Fraser University, Vancouver, Canada, where he works as an ethnographer with Maple Ridge Environmental School Project. He loves being active and still in the outdoors.

Jerry Tracey used to be head of an outdoor centre, but he now works as a high-school supply teacher when not out kayaking. He is also doing part-time research towards a PhD with the Outdoor Education section at Moray House, University of Edinburgh.

Peter Varley is director of the Centre for Recreation and Tourism Research, based in Fort William in the highlands of Scotland. Prior to this he was head of the School of Adventure Studies at the same institution, and before this a senior lecturer in

Marketing in Manchester. His PhD in sociology focused on the paradoxical commodification of adventure, with a particular focus on sea-kayaking courses. Current work includes papers on the liminal world of the adventurer, ecosophical approaches to tourism management, and the concept of 'slow' adventure.

Johnny Weinstock is a youth worker specializing in outdoor education. He is secretary of the Institute for Outdoor Learning (East region) and has published papers suggesting methods for improving and measuring the effectiveness of outdoor adventure.

Amanda West is a principal lecturer in the Department of Sport and Exercise Sciences at the University of Sunderland. Her PhD examined how risk mediated rock climbers' identities and reasons for climbing. She is a reviewer for the Higher Education Academy Awards for National Teaching Fellows. Her main outdoor adventures involved Munro-bagging and some gentle rock climbing.

Robyn Zink is an independent researcher whose research interests include questions associated with meaning, ethics and relationships with self and others. She continues to find Foucault's work very productive in exploring these things.

1

OUTDOOR ADVENTURE AND SOCIAL THEORY

Simon Beames and Elizabeth C.J. Pike

Consider all of the conversations that you've had with friends, colleagues, and family members in the last week. These conversations have taken place in kitchens, offices, parks, cafés, buses, bars, and locker rooms. To a certain extent, most of these encounters have involved people trying to make sense of their lives by sharing their perspectives and opinions with each other. This sense-making is a natural, normal part of human life.

Unfortunately, however, analyses of our social world are often limited by our (in)ability to arrive at a balanced and considered interpretation of what is happening around us and how it came to be. Sometimes we are left with having an opinion about something that affects our life that is not based on any robust, systematic examination of the surrounding circumstances. While this may not worry some, others may be searching for a way to help them understand the intricacies and complexities of human social existence at a much deeper level. That 'something' is social theory.

At its most fundamental level, the principal aim of this book is to enable readers to more rigorously interpret why people think and act in certain ways. As the title suggests, we'll use examples and scenarios from the world of outdoor adventure to illustrate how social theory can help us make greater sense of what's going on around us, in all facets of our lives.

Some assumptions

As editors of this book, we have made some assumptions about you, the reader. You have probably made some assumptions about the book's content and, perhaps, about the contributing writers. Let's get these assumptions out in the open, shall we?

We assume that you are a university student, field instructor, or lecturer involved in some form of outdoor leadership, adventure education, tourism and recreation management, or sport and leisure studies. We assume that you have an interest in outdoor and adventurous activities, such as canoeing, backpacking or climbing. We also suspect that you are not really interested in a book on social theory, as the content sounds rather dry and boring. Finally, we're almost certain that you'd rather be out doing some kind of outdoor adventure than be indoors, reading about it.

Thinking about who you are is one thing, but thinking about who you think we are is even trickier. So, we won't try that! As editors, we can tell you that every one of the contributors to this book knows some things about the world of outdoor adventure and about social theory. While no one author is an expert in all things adventurous and theoretical, each writer is an outdoor enthusiast of some kind (e.g. a paddler or skier) and each is an academic who has read, thought, obsessed, and written about how adventurous activities can be more deeply considered, analysed, and interpreted.

Clarification of terms

Before going any further it's necessary to clarify two main terms that we'll be using a lot: outdoor adventure and social theory. It's important to ensure that when we say 'outdoor adventure', we all attach a similar meaning to the term. The word 'outdoor' is easy enough; it's an adjective that refers to the open air, and is obviously the opposite of 'indoor'. Having said that, some of the chapters in this book will also discuss the movement indoors of what have been traditionally considered 'outdoor' activities – indoor climbing is an obvious example.

The meaning of the word 'adventure', however, is somewhat contested and not so easy to define. Hopkins and Putnam (1993) suggest that adventure can be described as 'an experience that involves uncertainty of outcome' (p. 6), while activities are usually defined as adventurous if they involve risk, challenge and inescapable consequences (Goldenberg, 2001). It is arguable that this book concerns risky, challenging and daring experiences that are usually performed outdoors, and this broad definition will probably have to suffice at a very basic level.

We'll add two caveats to this understanding, however. First, most of the adventures to which we are referring are those that can be considered outdoor 'lifestyle sports' (see Wheaton, 2004). Without this qualification, activities such as stealing cars and spray-painting graffiti on the side of a train could be considered outdoor adventure. After all, to some, these are 'challenging' and 'daring' outdoor activities that involve a certain amount of risk. This brings us to our second caveat: the meanings that individuals attach to certain activities are relative. So, what one person deems adventurous may not be to another person. An example of this is how some traditional alpinists think that bolted rock climbing is not adventurous because much of the risk of hurting oneself from a fall has been eliminated (and so it is not really dangerous or daring). Others think that there is plenty of adventure inherent in this kind of sport climbing; indeed, getting to the top is not guaranteed, a fall of two or three metres is quite common, and changing environmental conditions will influence a climber's success. We can say, then, that the amount of adventure inherent in a given activity is relative to the participant.

Another way of seeing outdoor adventure activities is as alternatives to mainstream Western sports (Rinehart, 2000; Wheaton, 2004). Although many adventurous sports are becoming formalized and commercialized through the X-games and the Olympics, these and other 'underground' activities (e.g. skateboarding and free-running) exist to a greater or lesser extent in contrast to the long-established sports of soccer in the UK, ice hockey in Canada, baseball in the USA, and rugby in New Zealand.

To be clear then, for the purposes of this book, outdoor adventure refers to lifestyle sports that have a certain degree of perceived excitement on behalf of the participant, exist as alternatives to mainstream sport, and which take place outdoors.

Next, let's turn our attention to defining 'social theory'. We understand 'social' as the organization and ways of life of people who interact with others within certain geographical, cultural, economic and political conditions. A 'theory' is a way of describing, analysing and explaining something – often with a view to reflecting on what has been learned and applying this knowledge to making change (see Coakley and Pike, 2009).

There are, of course, many different social theories, and all of these can be studied within the discipline of *social theory*. You will have heard the term *sociology*, which has a slightly different meaning to that of social theory. Generally speaking, there are sociologies of different topics, such as ageing, leisure, deviance, and sport. For example, the International Sociological Association has 55 research committees and eight groups that each focus on a different sociological area. These sociological examinations may draw on a number of social theories to help explain specific issues.

What does social theory have to do with outdoor adventure?

At this point, despite being clear on the two key terms, you may still be wondering what social theory has to do with outdoor adventure. Well, it probably won't surprise you to read that we think that social theory has everything to do with outdoor adventure! Let us explain.

What do going ski touring with two friends, taking an introduction to white-water kayaking course, or competing in an adventure race have in common? Well, besides the fact that they fit our definition of outdoor adventure, they all take place in the company of others; they are social affairs. The mere 'practice' of outdoor adventure is only one part of its social element. There are countless other related features that are social and which exert great influence on participants. Some examples of these influences include the media, equipment and clothing manufacturers, official sport governing bodies, family and friends, and customs/traditions. All five of these examples can be used to show how society shapes individuals' adventurous practices. This explains how solo adventurers are still influenced by social factors, even if they are walking to the South Pole on their own!

As we can see then, it is perhaps naive to think that the practice of outdoor adventurous activities is all about the activity. The ways in which adventurous activities are practised by participants are significantly influenced by numerous and varied social factors. We would argue that it is impossible to arrive at any deep understanding of outdoor adventure activities without examining the social forces that enable and constrain the behaviour of its participants.

Social theory isn't just helpful for understanding different kinds of outdoor adventures; it enables us to find deeper meanings in all kinds of ideas and practices that are part of our daily lives, such as education, politics, religion, leisure, and employment. In plain terms, our social worlds shape what we think and what we do. Part of being human is to try to understand the world in which we live (Craig and Beedie, 2010). Indeed, as noted earlier, when people converse at cafés, in kitchens, and at climbing walls, they are often trying to make sense of their 'worlds'. The trouble is that, without an adequate knowledge of social theory and its language, attempts to understand our social lives may be limited to what our colleague John Kelly calls 'pub chat'.

This book offers different theoretical perspectives that will (hopefully) provide you with new ways of seeing familiar practices. With this increased knowledge, you should, at the very least, become more aware of the ways in which you influence your social world and how it influences you.

Before we get into the meat of the book, there are some social theory basics of which we should all be aware. While not quite a course in Social Theory 101, the next section of this chapter looks at basic concepts and questions that will help you get more out of your chapter readings.

Social theory basics: the least you need to know

Studying the organization of society is something that people have been doing on an informal basis since humans have been humans. The actual formal study of society is quite young, however – just shy of 150 years old. Although the Frenchman Auguste Comte is widely regarded as being the founder of sociology in the late 1800s, it is scholars such as Durkheim, Marx and Weber who helped lay the theoretical foundations for the discipline. These writers and others found much material for their theorizing during the industrial revolution at the end of the nineteenth century, as this period in history involved tremendous changes in the social organization of work, family, and leisure.

From its French and German roots in classical theorists like Durkheim, Marx, and Weber, the development and use of social theory feature in most academic institutions around the world. While new theoretical concepts do emerge, it is arguable that much research is applied and involves using existing theory to interpret social circumstances that have been under-examined. This kind of theoretical examination is available to all of us – it's not just for those in ivory towers! Before tackling the chapters that follow, we believe that there are three main points of which all aspiring social theorists should be aware.

First, *all social theories offer explanations of how society influences individuals and how individuals can influence society*. While media, government, and peer groups shape what we think and do, so too are we able to shape them. Different theories have their own ways of accounting for this recursive relationship of society and individuals simultaneously influencing each other. Some social theories pay more attention to the *structural* features of society than to those of individual *agency* and vice versa. Structural features of society can be big, such as a national government, or small, like a typical family of four. These features can be formal rules or laws, or they can be informal, as in the *norms* that 'regulate' what people wear at posh restaurants. Agency is an easier term, since it simply refers to the power that people have to shape their social world. We all have some degree of agency in each of our different social arrangements.

This tension between the 'macro' (society's structures) and the 'micro' (society's individuals) is regarded by most social theorists as an inherent part of human life. Indeed, many would argue that within these tensions lie the most fascinating debates and discussion. A good question to ask yourself while reading and considering different scenarios throughout the book is: *how does social structure constrain and enable individual agency?*

The second point is that *there is not one 'best' social theory*. Put another way, there is no one 'super theory' that adequately explains every possible kind of social arrangement (although some theorists have tried!). What we can argue with greater conviction, however, is that for each set of circumstances – be it small office groups, little league baseball teams or seniors' residences – *there may be a particular theory that is especially useful* for understanding how these specific social circumstances have come to be.

The final point that we believe should be considered when appraising the usefulness of any social theory or theoretical framework is one of *equalities*. We need to ask *how the theory accounts for the ways in which certain people in society are more or less advantaged by the written rules, laws, and policies and the unwritten norms of behaviour.* How do these theories explain who has made the rules, why they are perpetuated, and how they can be changed?

Organization of the book

As noted earlier, this book does not explicate grand, over-arching, all-inclusive theories. Rather, each of the chapters features a specific *theoretical framework* and uses a particular adventurous activity to illustrate the concepts within it. A theoretical framework is a structure with boundaries used to understand, explain, and give meaning to the inter-related concepts that affect a phenomenon (Ennis, 1999). This book introduces a series of theoretical frameworks. The chapter on Marx, for example, does not seek to provide a summary of everything written by the great thinker. Instead, two of Marx's concepts are presented (alienation and false consciousness) and then brought alive with examples from the world of adventure tourism.

This structure is followed for the first two parts of the book. In the third part, each chapter uses a framework that draws on a number of scholars and which addresses a particular social issue, such as feminism, the ageing population, globalization, and climate change.

Part I outlines the work of three seminal thinkers in social theory: Karl Marx, Emile Durkheim and Max Weber. Marx's ideas surrounding *alienation* and *false consciousness* are brought to life by Carl Cater and Greg Dash. Chapter 2 uses examples from the New Zealand world of adventure tourism to explore the degree to which people are aware of how much they are buying into a highly commodified and manipulated activity. The authors also consider the circumstances that have contributed to the adventure tourism industry being developed and, naturally, why people might choose to go bungy jumping or white-water rafting in the first place.

In Chapter 3, Mike Brown focuses primarily on Durkheim's concept of the *collective conscience*. He uses the example of a single-handed around-the-world sailor, who uses promotional materials to try to connect observers and supporters with broader Scottish culture.

Chapter 4 features Max Weber's notions of rationalization, bureaucratization and control. Here, Peter Varley examines how so much of our adventuring tends to be constrained by space, time and formal rules. Examples of sport national governing bodies are employed to highlight how the development of training schemes, handbooks, and written policies all conspire to govern how canoeists and kayakers behave. Ultimately, the chapter asks if these forces of rationalization are diluting our own quests for adventure.

The second part comprises six chapters and introduces concepts by theorists in more recent times – although our first two writers, Gramsci and Elias, both conceived their seminal ideas as far back as the 1930s. Jerry Tracey starts this part by using Antonio Gramsci's notion of *hegemony* to investigate the ways in which informal, sociable playboating has evolved into competitive, freestyle kayaking. Tracey explains how this evolution of an adventurous activity has been driven by capitalism, yet widely accepted by those who might have resisted it.

Michael Atkinson's chapter explores the world of Parkour through Norbert Elias' concepts of the *civilizing process* and *mimesis*. Atkinson draws on Elias' work to show how activities such as Parkour (and or participation in them) do not happen in the absence of long-term (and often fascinating) histories.

Ken McCulloch's interest in sail training is given a theoretical interrogation by Erving Goffman's landmark essay on 'Total Institutions'. Here (Chapter 7) McCulloch considers how physical boundaries play a vital role in helping the institution achieve its aims. In the case of sail training, the boundaries inherent in not being able to leave the ship during its passage are of fundamental importance to creating the desired feeling of independence and self-sufficiency within the participants.

The eighth chapter is written by Simon Beames and John Telford. Here the fictional tale of two aspiring rock climbers is deconstructed using three of Pierre Bourdieu's conceptual gifts to the body of social theory: *habitus, capital* and *field.* Bourdieu's work is especially helpful in demonstrating how the 'rules' of climbing are shaped by those possessing various forms of capital.

Chapter 9 features the work of Anthony Giddens. Paul Beedie illustrates how elements of Giddens' *structuration theory* can be used as tools to analyse mountaineering practice. Beedie explains how activities ranging from indoor climbing to first ascents in the greater ranges have evolving resources and rules that both constrain and give us freedom in how we can behave.

The final chapter of Part II highlights the work of Michel Foucault. Robyn Zink employs Foucault's concepts of *power, surveillance* and *governmentality*, to assist us in understanding how challenge courses (aka aerial ropes courses) have become a widely accepted part of outdoor adventure education practice. Foucault's approach would have us first 'back up a step' and question how whatever we see as being 'true' about challenge course practice has come to be seen as the truth.

Part III of the book moves away from the format used in the first two parts and explores topics in outdoor adventure through bodies of literature, rather than through the eyes of one single theorist. Linda Allin and Amanda West start this part with an examination of female outdoor instructors. They show how the small proportion of female outdoor instructors can be examined through four different *feminist* perspectives.

Chapter 12, by Elizabeth Pike and Johnny Weinstock, draws on critical interactionism to explore how participating in outdoor adventurous activities can shape an older person's identity. The analysis highlights how people can come to view themselves as outdoor adventurers rather than as individuals who are ageing and perhaps have a disability.

The next chapter of Part III concentrates on *globalization* and how market forces and big business are influencing the kinds of adventures in which we are participating. Chris Loynes reveals how, in this era of late modernity, outdoor adventure practice from one culture can be replicated and exported to another – often across national boundaries.

With climate change being arguably the biggest threat to human life, it is appropriate to have the final chapter focus on *low-carbon adventure*. Kate Rawles discusses how the kinds of adventures on which we embark need to shift towards ones with a less detrimental impact on climate change and bio-diversity.

The book is organized in such a way that it doesn't have to be read in chronological order. Readers can choose to read particular chapters that interest them, without fear of having missed a key piece of information from the chapter before.

Finally, two specific limitations of this book need to be acknowledged. First, we are only introducing a small number of social theorists; there are many well-known and influential sociologists who do not feature. This is an introductory text, after all, and while we have included many seminal thinkers, we haven't been able to give space to everyone we might have liked to. Second, and related to this first point, there are myriad issues and topics that we could have chosen for Part III. Consider the 2010 UK Equalities Act, for example, which identifies nine characteristics that cannot be used as reasons to treat people unfairly. As with the theorists, we couldn't look at all of these marginalized populations, and so a number have been left out.

Closing

We've now explored some assumptions about you, us, and the book; defined some terms; and outlined key points to remember when reading the chapters. We close this introduction by sharing our hopes for this book.

Our aim is for readers of this book to:

a   move away from using 'pub chat' as their principal means of making sense of social aspects of outdoor adventure;
b   examine outdoor adventure through different theoretical perspectives, angles, and lenses;
c   consider how outdoor adventure may disadvantage some people and privilege others;
d   explore the role that outdoor adventure does/does not/could play within society; and
e   ensure that policies and practices are informed by theory.

We hope to see you again in Chapter 15, where we will revisit these aims and discuss how we can more deeply consider the 'so what?' questions that probably emerged during your reading.

Further reading

For accessible introductory reading on social theory and sociology, consider Coakley and Pike (referenced below) and the following sources:

Jones, P. (2010) *Introducing social theory*, Cambridge: Polity Press.
Layder, D. (2005) *Understanding social theory* (2nd edn), London: Sage.
Swingewood, A. (2000) *A Short History of Sociological Thought* (3rd edn), Basingstoke: Palgrave Macmillan.

References

Coakley, J. and Pike, E. (2009) *Sports in society: Issues and controversies,* London: McGraw-Hill.
Craig, P. and Beedie, P. (2010) *Sport sociology* (2nd edn), Exeter: Learning Matters.
Ennis, C.D. (1999) 'The theoretical framework: The central piece of a research plan', *Journal of Teaching in Physical Education*, 18, 129–40.
Goldenberg, M. (2001) *Outdoor and risk educational practices*, Washington, DC: ERIC Clearinghouse.

Hopkins, D. and Putnam, R. (1993) *Personal growth through adventure*, London: David Fulton.

Rinehart, R. (2000) 'Emerging arriving sports: Alternatives to formal sports', in J. Coakley and E. Dunning (eds), *Handbook of sports studies* (pp. 501–20), London: Sage.

Wheaton, B. (ed.) (2004) *Understanding lifestyle sports: Consumption, identity and difference*, London: Routledge.

PART I

Classical sociological interpretations of outdoor adventure

2

KARL MARX

Alienation and false consciousness in adventurous activities

Carl Cater and Greg Dash

> Sie wissen das nicht, aber sie tun es [they do not know it, but they are doing it]
>
> *(Karl Marx,* Capital, *vol. 1)*

It could be argued that Karl Marx, of all the social theorists, and his writings have had the most significant impact on the world. His concerns with the class struggle indirectly led to the communist revolutions of the early twentieth century and shaped the course of history for much of that century. Although his political relevance has perhaps declined with the 'victory' of capitalism and free markets, the current global economic crisis shows that Marx's teachings are still highly relevant to how we consider consumption practices. In the modern era of commercial outdoor adventure in which we can buy experiences and equipment, his work becomes increasingly informative. This chapter will consider Marx's ideas of *alienation* and *false consciousness* in relation to outdoor adventure, and use examples from adventure tourism in New Zealand, with a particular emphasis on the Kiwi 'sport' of bungy jumping. Before discussing Marx's work, we shall look at the period when Marx was writing, as this is critical to understanding his theories.

Biography

Karl Marx was born in 1818 in Trier, Germany, and studied in Bonn and Berlin, before moving to Paris in 1843, where he met his future collaborator Friedrich Engels. Here he wrote *The Economic and Philosophical Manuscripts of 1844*, in which he introduced the concept of alienation (Marx, 1844/1959). In 1848 he moved to London, where he published *The Communist Manifesto* and, later, his three part work on human society and economics, *Capital* (1867). Marx was particularly intrigued by the struggle he saw between the *proletariat* class (the majority of people, who were the workers producing material goods) and the *bourgeoisie* class (the elite, those who owned and exploited the means of production). The nineteenth century was a time of huge advances in the development of Western societies, with the effects of industrialization bringing huge benefits, but also great inequalities, to the people living in these countries.

It is unlikely that Karl Marx would have called himself a philosopher. Indeed, he was critical of philosophy in his own writing, declaring that 'the philosophers have only interpreted the world, in various ways; the point, however, is to change it' (Feuer, 1969, p. 286). Through his work, Marx aimed to develop an understanding of the world that could bring about social and intellectual revolution (although this was only to happen after his death in 1883). Marx is better referred to as an 'anti-philosopher' (Eagleton, 1997), as he rejected the metaphysical questions of traditional philosophy to focus on more fundamental questions of power, difference and being, or in Marx's case 'historical conditions'.

Marx emerged from a group of radical thinkers known as the 'young Hegelians', who adopted Hegel's dialectical method (which considers that everything in the world is made up of opposites) but rejected his philosophy of idealism. Instead, Marx was influenced by the work of the Greek philosopher Epicurus and was prompted to adopt a philosophical position of materialism, which sees the constantly changing arrangements of nature itself as the basis on which ideas are formed. For Marx, consciousness (or what we say and what we think) is ultimately determined by our actions. The material reality of the world is more fundamental than ideas that come from it, and it gives rise to the cultural, legal, political and ideological 'superstructure' that governs ideas. Thus, what we think and what we desire are bound up in the social and political world around us.

Adventure tourism can be considered just like any other commodity, as it is determined by the social and political world that promotes it. This notion is the basis of Marx's theory of historical materialism. It views 'consciousness' not as the product of circumstance (like molecules coming together as per the laws of physics), but rather as a product of the historical conditions within which they emerge. This kind of thinking allows theoretical problems to be solved outside of philosophy and highlights the potential for social transformation through politics. Marx (1974, p. 59) stated that history is 'a sum of productive forces, an historical created relation of individuals to nature and to one another, which is handed down to each generation from its predecessor . . . It shows that circumstances make men[*sic*] just as men[*sic*] make circumstances.'

Alienation

The above quotation on humans being 'made' by circumstances suggests that humans have a certain lack of control over their thoughts. Marx explained this by developing the concept of alienation or estrangement, where something (particularly ourselves) is separated from, or strange to, something else. On one hand, we could argue that the desire for adventure is partly a response to feeling alienated from ourselves and society. In our everyday working lives much of what we pursue may seem meaningless and mundane, so we seek to re-engage with nature, both the external nature of the natural world and the internal nature comprising our bodies and feelings (see Cater and Smith, 2003). However, in order to do this we are increasingly turning to commercial adventure activity providers who can give us these experiences in a packaged format. These experiences appear at first to offer a fulfilling experience, but they never truly give us an authentic experience and so we are always desiring more. Take, for example, this quotation from a prominent British newspaper:

> Most people don't have the time or want to reach a level of independent competence in many activities, so in effect they go shopping for the expertise, buying in experience, handing the duty of care to someone who does have the right certificate or training.
>
> *(Guardian, G2, 28 July 1999, p. 3)*

The marketplace is where we shop for *things* (and increasingly experiences). Marx felt that the way this marketplace operates hides the actual work and time spent by people involved in making these things. In the marketplace, economic values of commodities are determined relative to each other and by their exchange value. These exchange values are then expressed in money and allow commodities to be traded. The exchange process in adventure tourism requires a trade of money for the skills and knowledge of the adventure provider. For Marx, money represents a distorted representation of the value an individual creates through labour. Money allows individuals to trade time spent working on different commodities, and thus represents a social relationship. The way the market operates distorts this relationship between money and labour time, as it alters the social processes that are involved in trade and alienates individuals from each other. Money becomes the alienated essence of labour and is described by Marx as being worshipped in a theological sense, while conferring power over its possessor. This drives a need for the accumulation of money and wealth and a desire to amass created goods.

In another sense, we could also argue that commercialization of adventure has meant that we are alienated further from real feelings and real experiences, as many commercial activities rely on a short, sharp dose of adrenaline-filled activity rather than on building skills and a genuine awareness of the environment. Take, for example, the bungy jump, which requires little or no skill and is an activity that will always feel 'strange'. Compare this to the years that might be invested in becoming a good climber or kayaker, and the deep spatial awareness of one's body that is required for these more dedicated pursuits (see Lewis, 2000; Varley, 2011), and the social relations that come with this. Here's what some bungy jumpers in New Zealand said about their experience, which illustrates this concept of alienation:

> *Completely alien, it's an alien experience . . . It's just . . . you can't really explain it can you? You've just got to go and do it.*
>
> *(Chris, UK, Kawarau Bungy)*

I felt fine, I really did. Honestly I don't remember too much. I think I was just, everything was kinda shutting down and yeah, I got out there on the edge and I just looked at it, and you know I think I just shut down all my regular senses. I couldn't remember what the music was until I saw the video . . . I totally just blanked out.

(Eric, USA, Pipeline Bungy)

Part of me seemed to be switched off, because there are parts of it I can't remember . . . I don't know, I'd like to think I was concentrating, but a lot of it just goes straight through your mind and you forget it.

(Adam, UK, Kawarau Bungy)

To some degree, then, it becomes difficult for adventure tourists to see the processes happening in bungy jumping as they are obscured by the operators. These people may actually become further alienated through their bungy jumping experience. Marx worried about this alienation that modern societies and structures encouraged, especially because he felt that most people were not aware that this alienation was occurring.

Ideology and false consciousness

Marx argues that in a class society with clear social divisions, precisely because the 'base' of social relations is unjust, the politics, law and ideology often serve to promote or conceal this injustice. The dominant ideology is referred to by Marx as the 'superstructure' and is controlled by the ruling class, as they have the means of production at their disposal. This dominant material relationship is expressed as ideas that function to the benefit of the ruling class, and the economic interests of the ruling class then become the economic interests of the entire society. If we look at the history of adventure, it has been dominated throughout time by the desires of the elite and the rich (Macfarlane, 2004), and yet the masses aspire to have the opportunities of the elite. Adventure has always been expensive in both time and money terms, so it is those with the resources and power who are most likely to do it.

This desirability of adventure is reinforced through media messages and reaches the wage labourer (aka proletariat) class as well as the ruling bourgeoisie. Here, the power of the dominant ideology offers promises of potential for upward mobility and personal achievement. Whether produced as a conscious effort by the dominant class, such as through advertising, or as an unconscious effort that is demanded by the material conditions, ideology represents the 'imaginary relationship of individuals to their real conditions of existence' (Althusser, 2001, p. 54). Indeed, it has often been said that it is easier to imagine the end of the world than it is to imagine the end of capitalism. Capitalism has become the frame through which society is viewed, so even when we try to overcome it, we think in its terms.

Although we could argue that outdoor adventure is a way of escaping the material world and getting 'back to nature', the commercialization of adventure activities has to some degree warped this relationship between material and natural worlds. This is particularly obvious with adventure equipment – the demand for which is driven heavily by advertising and the media. Riley (1995, p. 634) explains this as the need to engage 'in ideal rather than utilitarian consumption; the burgeoning phenomenon of fashion-oriented consumption; and an increase of interpreted symbolism from consumptive displays'. Thus, a huge consumer goods industry has grown alongside outdoor recreation, with goods that 'possess qualities beyond their functional purpose' (Riley, 1995, p. 634), and with brands such as the North Face becoming as popular on the high street as in the mountains. Similarly, Johnston and Edwards (1994, p. 468) have demonstrated how the activity of mountaineering has become progressively commodified:

> Corporate sponsorship has shaped mountain experiences and even the fantasy of a mountain experience in order to sell commodities to a consuming culture. [As a result] . . . many more well-equipped, stylishly dressed holiday consumers are travelling to mountain regions . . . sent by an ever-growing legion of adventure travel companies who advertise their services in [an also growing number] of 'Adventure Travel' magazines and guides. They arrive carrying clothing and equipment purchased at outdoor shops staffed by adventure enthusiasts; and they are guided through their mountain adventure by mountaineers turned tour guides.

This quotation illustrates how the 'adventuring proletariat' are complicit in their supporting role: they are literally buying into it. Marx argued that the ideological control of the dominant class results in what is referred to as a 'false consciousness' of the proletariat. That is, they believe they are acting in their own interests but are instead acting to the benefit of capital. Although the theory was developed by Marx, the term 'false consciousness' was used by later scholars to describe this 'inability to see things, especially social relations and relations of exploitation as they really are' (Blackburn, 1994, p. 135).

Processes that lead to false consciousness may be exacerbated in adventure tourism, where the public need for an authentic adventure experience is the driving force that is encouraging the industry to be progressively more commodified. It is suggested that, from a principled viewpoint, commercial interest and adventure are opposed, and careful masking of this relationship takes place. This leads to a situation where operators of adventurous activity businesses will 'adopt tried and tested techniques of branding, marketing, pricing, ancillary product sales, safety, staff performance and the like', as described by Cloke and Perkins (2002, p. 546). For example, it is interesting to see how, for many adventure tourism operators, souvenirs, such as T-shirts, are positioned as just as much a form of advertising, and therefore product reinforcement, as they are a business venture in themselves:

> *Advertising is the main thing with the merchandise, there isn't a great mark-up on the t-shirts to be honest, because they get seen around the world and people go 'oh what is that?' . . . it sells for us.*

> (Marketing manager, Pipeline Bungy)

This form of marketing creates a desire to engage in these adventurous activities because they are cool, as 'experiences of adventure have emerged as increasingly desired and fashionable commodities' (Cater and Smith, 2003, p. 195), even though participants are not fully conscious of why that is so. Marx would suggest that elements of adventure may then become *fetishized*, which means that they are worshipped for their almost magical qualities. In *On the Fetishism of Commodities* (in *Capital*, 1867), Marx argued that, under capitalism, commodities take on a life of their own – a fetishistic quality – as the transactions between them begin to govern human relations, rather than the other way around. This might sound rather primitive, but one only needs to consider that the original idea of bungy jumping came from the ritual land divers of Pentecost in the Pacific. While these Pacific islanders perform a ritual of diving off towers with vines attached to their legs in blessing a good yam harvest and proving their male virility, modern tourists seek to travel the world to embark on similarly ritualistic bungy experiences in exchange for money.

> *We thought it was the thing you did in New Zealand anyway, everyone who . . . As soon as I knew I was going to go to New Zealand I knew I was going to jump, because everyone who has been here has said that you have got to do it you know?*
>
> *(Charlotte, UK, 15–25, Kawarau Bungy)*

This fetishism can also be seen in the importance of the height of a bungy jump in advertising. This often forms an important part of the attraction for a significant proportion of participants:

> *I was deciding that if I was going to jump I wanted to do the 71m, I didn't want to do a small one, if I jump I want to JUMP! I wanted something higher so it would mean something.*
>
> *(Naya, Israel, 15–25, A.J. Hackett)*

The marketing manager of the Pipeline Bungy in Queenstown confirmed the importance of the jump's height and highlighted how the very numbers themselves become icons that are then imbued into the performance of the activity.

Narratives and theming of activities are also recognized as highly important processes in adventure tourism, particularly in a commercially competitive environment. A clear theme helps to distinguish an activity from its competitors, and this can be seen in the obvious branding of the Pipeline bungy jump. Here, the rebuilding of a fake gold sluicing pipe across the gorge, harking back to local industry a century before, defines the frontier gold-rush element to the Pipeline experience. So successful has this piece of adventure architecture become that few participants realize the actual inauthenticity of the icon. Such a process may be presented as an example of what Hollinshead (1998) terms a 'distory' in tourist practice, which is the selective presentation of history in a commodified and manipulated fashion. Such practices involve a 'seizure of useable storylines from the past which are decontextualised and romanticised and thereby turned into nostalgia which can decorate, and be purchased, but are frequently much diminished in connected meaning' (p. 80). Thus, the playful expression of adventure creates a false representation of history in tourist consciousness.

Of course, a very significant area where relationships are obscured in adventure (and hence where there is false consciousness) is in risk management. As Cater (2006) has shown, perceived risk in adventure tourism is manipulated as a product to sell, while real risk is managed in order to make the activity as safe (and commercially viable) as possible. Varley (2006) explains this phenomenon as the 'adventure com-modification continuum', where he argues that there is the greatest amount of business in activities where risk can be managed out of the pursuit. These are also those activities that can be the most commodified, and so to which Marxian concepts are most applicable. Bungy jumping is perhaps the best example of this manipulation of risk, as there is very little actual risk at well-managed sites.

> *Oh they have no idea, it's all perceived risk, and it's way out.*
>
> *(Stu, jumpmaster, A.J. Hackett)*

> *Well the actual risk is zero, it's minimal because there is no risk at all, it is perceived, and perception is reality.*
>
> *(Mark, driver/guide, A.J. Hackett)*

Yet because of its direct challenge to gravity, participants see bungy jumping as an activity where there is a higher degree of risk:

> *I suppose there is no risk in bungy jumping, but I see that as a fairly huge risk so I won't do it.*
>
> *(Kevin, Australia, Shotover Jet)*

We can see that this is a false consciousness manipulated by the providers, as many participants want some sensation of perceived risk in order to feel adrenaline and excitement. As Cater (2006) has shown, this is often carefully managed for individual clients through guides' assessments of the relative need of individuals to feel scared, in something he terms the *fear paradox*. This is a paradox because those who are often the most scared need to be reassured and made to feel safe, while those who are the least scared require an illusion of risk in order to feel excited.

> *I think people come with an inherent fear factor, and what they like doing is pushing themselves above that. And the really interesting thing is, especially with bungy, is that people with high fear thresholds, i.e. they can withstand a lot of fear, basically get very little out of the bungy, it is something that they can do no problem. People with a low threshold and naturally very scared have a huge rush, as they have really had to get over and conquer some pretty serious fear to go and do it. It is amazing the number of people that will tell you that the bungy was a life changing thing, they really do feel that they have conquered something.*
>
> *(Marketing manager, rafting operator)*

In addition to this feeling of individual conquest within mass adventure tourism, there is also a degree of Marxian false consciousness in the wearing of clothing and gear during adventure activities that may not be strictly necessary for safety purposes. It is clear that in the performance of adventure there is often the requirement to feel that the participant is wearing suitable attire for the experience. So, the donning of specific *costumes* – or, in some cases, the removal of more 'ordinary' ones, as in the relatively common practice of bungy jumping naked or just in underwear – is a clearly performative aspect of the practice. One of the operators of a jetboat ride showed how these notions of 'looking the part' or like the classic adventurer work:

> *The lifejackets are really just for the photos, I mean yes they would make you float if you did fall out of the boat, but we don't let people fall out of the boat. So the lifejacket is part of the . . . It's part of the experience you know.*
>
> *(Marketing Manager, jetboat ride)*

Conclusion

It is clear that there are Marxian elements of alienation, ideology and false consciousness in adventure tourism – particularly in more commercial activities such as bungy jumping. There is alienation from the skills that are required should we want to become independent adventurers. There is commercialized ideology in the marketing and advertising of adventure products and adventure activities – for example, in outdoor clothing and in the display inherent in 'adventure fashion'. There is false consciousness in the narratives of adventure and the feeling of risk. Most of all, we could argue that there is false consciousness in the very desire for adventure, which is perpetrated as 'the thing' for us to do in our holiday and leisure time. The next time you are engaging in an adventurous activity, whether individually or commercially, see if there are elements of false consciousness – in branding, commentaries or risk evaluations. Where does your need for adventure really come from? How is money (and value) exchanged in our outdoor adventures?

However, should we be so critical of the desire for commercial adventure? Marx's ideas have received as much critique as they have praise in the contemporary era, as, despite continuing inequalities between the classes, the differences in twenty-first-century democratic societies are far less stark than those of the nineteenth century. Concepts of power and structures are still relevant, but we are much more critical as consumers than Marx might have us believe. Many of us may feel that we are fully aware of how commodified the world is, and we use these structures to allow us to express ourselves in a playful manner. However, we may also want to consider the degree to which we are able to operate outside of these structures. In the practice of adventure, perhaps we should be looking at some of the other social theorists who are examined in this book, as they might do more to celebrate human leisure engagement with the outdoors.

Certainly the growth of adventure tourism has as much to do with our desire to play as adults. Indeed, it has been found that adventure activities are normally ranked much higher in tourist satisfaction than other areas of the holiday experience, because of their playful character and because they are fundamentally about pleasure and fun (Cater and Smith, 2003). It should be clear that we can learn a great deal about ourselves through such engagement, but to ignore the importance of hedonism is to miss the principal aim of these pursuits: 'What price a ripe old age in the sterilised bubble, when there is the temptation of adventure on the outside and a short sharp dose of Life?' (Eassom, 1993, p. 27).

Adventure tourism, and bungy jumping in particular, are symbols for the post-modern touristic mode and, as such, expressions of tourism in the twenty-first century. In our speeded-up, hyper-real global village, we are increasingly encour-aged to 'jump right in' and try all that is (commercially) offered at the smorgasbord of experience. Perhaps, then, we should update the Marx quotation from the beginning of the chapter and emphasise that participants 'do know it, but are doing it anyway!'.

Further reading

There are few examples of Marxian application to outdoor adventure, as most of his writing was directed at the urban class struggle. However, Greenwood (1989) shows how Marxian concepts can be applied to ideas of authenticity and com-modification of tourist places. For a Nietzschean interpretation of adventure tourism see Cater (2007). Given the huge influence of Marx on politics and social sciences, there are many introductory texts. Some have cartoons (e.g. Rius, 2003), and others are more comprehensive (e.g. Sitton, 2012). Many of Marx's original ideas are contained within the brief *Communist manifesto* (referenced below), which is easier to read than his later works, as it was designed to be read by common folk.

Cater, C. (2007) 'Adventure tourism: Will to power?', in A. Church and T. Coles (eds), *Tourism, power and space* (pp. 63–82), London: Routledge.
Greenwood, D. (1989) 'Culture by the pound: An anthropological perspective on tourism as cultural commoditization', in V. Smith (ed.), *Hosts and guests: The anthropology of tourism* (pp. 171–86), Philadelphia, PA: University of Pennsylvania Press.
Rius, J. (2003) *Marx for beginners*, London: Pantheon.
Sitton, J.F. (ed.) (2012) *Marx today: Selected works and recent debates*, Oxford: Palgrave Macmillan.

References

Althusser, L. (2001) *Lenin and philosophy and other essays*, trans. B. Brewster, New York: Monthly Review Press.
Blackburn, S. (1994) *The Oxford dictionary of philosophy*, Oxford: Oxford University Press.
Cater, C. (2006) 'Playing with risk? Participant perceptions of risk and management implications in adventure tourism', *Tourism Management*, 27(2), 317–25.
Cater, C. and Smith, L. (2003) 'New country visions: Adventurous bodies in rural tourism', in P. Cloke (ed.), *Country visions* (pp. 195–215), Oxford: Pearson.

Cloke, P. and Perkins, H.C. (2002) 'Commodification and adventure in New Zealand tourism', *Current Issues in Tourism*, 5, 521–49.

Eagleton T. (1997) *Marx*, London: Orion.

Eassom, S. (1993) 'Leisure, health and happiness: In praise of hedonism', in C. Brackenridge (ed.), *Body matters: Leisure images and lifestyles* (pp. 32–49), Brighton: Leisure Studies Association.

Feuer, L.S. (ed.) (1969) *Marx and Engels: Basic writings on politics and philosophy*, London: Anchor.

Guardian (1999) 'Criticism grows of disaster gorge trip' *Guardian*, G2, 28 July, p. 3.

Hollinshead, K. (1998) 'Disney and commodity aesthetics: A critique of Fjellman's analysis of "Distory" and the "Historicide" of the past', *Current Issues in Tourism*, 1(1), 58–119.

Johnston, B.R. and Edwards, T. (1994) 'The commodification of mountaineering', *Annals of Tourism Research*, 21, 459–77.

Lewis, N. (2000) 'The climbing body, nature and the experience of modernity', *Body and Society*, 6(3–4), 58–80.

Macfarlane, R. (2004) *Mountains of the mind: A history of a fascination*, London: Granta.

Marx, K. (1844/1959) *The economic and philosophical manuscripts of 1844*, Moscow: Progress Publishers.

Marx, K. (1867) *Capital: Critique of political economy*, Chicago, IL: Charles H. Kerr and Co.

Marx, K. (1974) *The German ideology*, ed. C.J. Arthur, London: Lawrence & Wishart.

Marx, K. and Engels, F. (1848) *The communist manifesto*, London: Pluto Press.

Riley, R. (1995) 'Prestige-worthy tourism behaviour', *Annals of Tourism Research*, 22, 630–49.

Varley, P.J. (2006) 'Confecting adventure and playing with meaning: The adventure commodification continuum', *Journal of Sport and Tourism*, 11(2), 173–94.

Varley, P.J. (2011) 'Sea kayakers at the margins: The liminoid character of contemporary adventures', *Leisure Studies*, 30(1), 85–98.

3

EMILE DURKHEIM

Structural functionalism, adventure and the social order

Mike Brown

Introduction

Emile Durkheim was one of the key influential thinkers in shaping the field of sociology. His investigations into many aspects of social life such as suicide, religion, industrialization and education – coupled with his efforts to establish sociology as an academic discipline – have had an enduring impact on the social sciences. There are many excellent introductory texts that cover Durkheim's life and works; therefore I see little point in presenting material covered elsewhere (for example, see Morrison, 1995; Swingewood, 2000; Jones, 2003). Rather, I want to focus on a key aspect of Durkheim's work: his quest to understand the 'glue' that held society together in the face of rising individualism. After briefly setting the scene and introducing his contribution to sociology, I will present an example of how his ideas might help us to understand adventure in modern society.

Biography

Emile Durkheim was born in 1858 into a family of modest means in a small rural town in France. His father, grandfather and great grandfather were rabbis. As a young man he contemplated entering into his father's vocation, but his pursuit of an academic career led him in a different and very secular direction. He lived during a turbulent period of French history, when great changes were being brought about by industrialization and political turmoil. His efforts to understand the nature of society, and how it continued to function in a relatively orderly and cohesive manner, were influenced by more than a desire to generate abstract theory; they were based on observations of the real world undergoing rapid upheaval.

It was as a student in Paris that Durkheim became interested in studying society and how it functioned. If it were possible to understand how a harmonious society operated, then attempts at social reform might be more successful. During his career he held academic positions at the University of Bordeaux and at the Sorbonne in Paris. In both institutions he taught a wide range of topics, which illustrates the breadth of his expertise. For example, in Bordeaux he taught papers in social solidarity, the family, moral education, suicide, criminology and religion (Hughes *et al.*, 1995).

Following his appointment at the Sorbonne in 1902, he became increasingly influential in the realm of education. He was an instrumental figure in establishing a national free and secular education system in France. He died in 1917, at the age of 59, following a stroke and the news of the death of his son in the First World War.

Key contributions

It is important to be aware of the social and political changes in France between 1870 and 1895 in order to better understand the intellectual and social climate in which Durkheim formulated his ideas. Some examples of these changes include France's defeat in the Franco-Prussian War, the fall of Napoleon III, and the establishment of the Third Republic. Durkheim was convinced that for sociology to be credible, and to make a difference in society, it needed to be based on scientific principles. It has been suggested that through sociology he sought to assist in 'the formulation of a new civic ethic, a modern republican ideology which rejected both traditional French Catholicism and a deeply entrenched social conservatism' (Swingewood, 2000, p. 57).

The identification of 'social facts'

Following Auguste Comte's promotion of the scientific methodology across all disciplinary areas, Durkheim sought to establish sociology as a distinct disciplinary area that could be studied with accepted scientific methods. In order to do this, he sought to align sociological methods with more established university disciplines by providing a reasoned explanation for how order is achieved in society and how social solidarity can be maintained in times of change. He believed that the key to understanding this problem lay in the relationship between the individual and society. Durkheim proposed that, to function smoothly, society relied on a *collective consciousness* or commonly held norms and values that determined collective behaviour. These 'structures' largely held individual desires in check and contributed to maintaining social order. An example might be the belief that risk-taking is an essential component of your national identity. Kane (2011) has illustrated how Sir Edmund Hillary's first ascent of Mount Everest reinforced adventure as a 'positively valued social tenet in New Zealand' (p. 1). Thus, in New Zealand, adventurers such as Sir Edmund Hillary are highly valued and their feats are publicly acclaimed. Seen this way, the collective consciousness of the value of risk-taking underpins collective behaviour.

Careful investigation of the collective consciousness revealed what Durkheim termed *social facts*. The case for social facts featured predominantly in two of his major works: *The Rules of Sociological Method* (1895/1938) and *Suicide* (1897/1970). The argument for the existence of 'social facts' was the central thrust of his examination of the distribution of suicide. The occurrence of suicide, and the collection of data regarding its frequency, allowed Durkheim to study it as a social phenomenon rather than view it as an individual act. Social facts can be thought of as 'social forces which are independent of individual control and which shape our destinies' (Giulianotti, 2005, p. 1). These influencing social facts of family, religion or professional group, for example, were considered to be objective social phenomena that were 'hidden from ordinary perception' (Swingewood, 2000, p. 58).

By arguing for social facts, Durkheim sought to move beyond individual explanations of human behaviour in order to understand how external forces influenced actions. These 'external forces' are society's norms and values that exist independently of individuals. This led Durkheim to argue that society was *sui generis* (1895/1938), which means that it could not be reduced to independent individual actions. From Durkheim's perspective, the distribution of particular social facts depended on the type of society in which people lived, rather than on particular personal dispositions. The role that the collective consciousness plays in determining individual behaviour features prominently in more recent sociological writings concerning the structure (society)–agency (individual) debate.

Social cohesion: the individual–society relationship

Concern with social cohesion in the face of increasing individualism, and the promotion of individual rights, were very much at the forefront of Durkheim's thinking. He considered that industrialization coupled with humans' inherent selfish desires promoted individualism over the collective good. Durkheim referred to this as the 'cult of the individual' (1893/1984, p. 338). The outcome of excessive individualism was collective and individual ill health, which resulted in what he termed *anomie*: 'the sense of normlessness and lower moral regulation among individuals' (Giulianotti, 2005, p. 2). In Durkheim's view, anomie, or 'the promotion of unrestricted desires' (Jones, 2003, p. 36), was harmful to the well-being of society. Hence, he sought to provide a reasoned alternative to counter this excessive individualism by trying to ensure that society could continue to function harmoniously. In the adventure context we can see how self-sacrifice, the opposite of a 'me first attitude', is highly valued. In contrast to anomie, adventurers often praise those who put the team or the success of an expedition above their own desires. Perhaps the most famous example is the act of Captain Oates in Scott's unsuccessful Antarctic expedition in 1912. Believing that he would hinder his team-mates' chances of survival due to his slow progress, Oates walked out of his tent into a blizzard and to his certain death.

The Division of Labour (1893/1984) was Durkheim's attempt to understand the nature of the links that connected the individual to society and the social bonds that linked individuals. More specifically, he was interested in the changes that occurred in these social links as society became more advanced and differentiated (Morrison,

1995). Industrialization and urbanization clearly resulted in increasing specialization and division in the workplace and the collapse of traditional community structures, yet modern society was not anarchic. In the face of these monumental changes, what was the glue that maintained social solidarity?

Durkheim held that society was essentially a system made up of interrelated moral relationships. These relationships are based on mutual and reciprocal expectations of behaviour. For example, if I am out sailing and am in distress, there is an expectation that other sailors would render all reasonable assistance if called upon. This understanding is common across most Western maritime cultures. There is, in Durkheim's terminology, a collective consciousness that is held by mariners. This example is a specific illustration of a wider collective consciousness that Durkheim argued was held by society more generally. Another example of a collective consciousness is religious belief. If religious beliefs are widespread, they may perform the function of unifying society. It is important to point out that Durkheim (1912/1995) was not interested in the causes of religious belief, nor claims to truth, but rather the function that religion played in maintaining social order. A collective consciousness constrains and obliges people to act in certain ways; it is a way of thinking or acting that permeates the collective and thus extends beyond the individual.

While industrialization had altered the conditions of employment and led to job specialization and a greater division of labour, resulting in little or no contact between groups of workers, society had not dramatically fallen apart. Durkheim (1912/1995) suggested that as society had moved from being organized around *mechanical solidarity* (an agrarian basis with little differentiation of labour), it had developed and adapted to a new form of solidarity based on interdependence, which he termed *organic solidarity*. Industrialization may have altered working patterns, but society continued to be underpinned by mutual and reciprocal expectations of behaviour that were a moral reality.

Durkheim's thesis concerning the role of collective norms and values as a moral reality sheds light on the processes of socialization. We are brought up through various social structures (e.g. family, school, church) that normalize certain ways of thinking and acting that we seldom question, for we consider them to be natural. On a daily basis we do not have to consciously think about most of our actions. It is only if we know that we are likely to contravene the collective consciousness that we may become aware of society's expectations. For example, if you chose not to participate in a rock-climbing session or canoeing trip as part of a camp experience, it is likely that you might have thought: 'what will my friends, camp leader, family think of me?'

Hopefully, this brief overview of Durkheim's ideas will stimulate some thoughts about the role of the collective consciousness in shaping society as we experience it today. It seems somewhat ironic, and a little bit quaint, to hear of Durkheim's concern with excessive individualism a century ago. The pace of technological advance has not slowed, and talk of the 'me' generation with its unbridled individualism continues to be a topic of discussion among contemporary educators, parents and employers. Western industrial society continues to function relatively harmoniously despite some rather large hiccups (e.g. two world wars, environmental degradation, the widening wealth gap). This suggests that, in Durkheim's terms, the mutual and reciprocal expectations of norms and values in society have provided a counterbalance to the forces that might lead to excessive individualism and anomie. Drawing on Durkheim's theory, I will now explain how adventure might function to maintain social cohesion in society.

Adventure and society

Unfortunately, Durkheim did not write specifically on the topic of adventure. So how might his overriding concern about the relationship between the individual and society help us to understand contemporary adventure and adventurers? It is tempting to think that adventurous or extreme sports participation can best be seen as a matter of individual choice and a means of self-gratification. Viewed this way we might ask: 'why do individuals take risks?' The question could possibly be answered via psychometric tests or personality profiles. As valuable as such approaches might be, they consign adventurous behaviour to matters of individual choice or personal dispositions. Such an approach fails to answer bigger questions concerning the role or function that adventure might perform in society. For example, why are adventurers newsworthy, why do we buy adventure books, and why do large corporations provide sponsorship for adventurers?

I suggest that the answers to these questions have much to do with the fact that society considers adventure as something of value – a value that is greater than the personal rewards that might be accrued by the individuals involved in an adventure. As a society we celebrate adventurers' achievements as 'our achievements' and claim that they reflect national values that we (supposedly) all hold dear. These adventurers are often held up as role models and often receive 'official' endorsements, such as knighthoods and other honorary titles. Durkheim's perspective may assist us to understand the social nature of the role of adventure and adventurers in society. In the following section I consider how the language surrounding a particular outdoor adventure conveys ideas that reinforce social solidarity and social order. This case study illustrates how media representations can act as part of the socialization process.

A global ocean race: adventure and a version of national identity

I wrote this chapter while in Edinburgh on study leave in early 2012. I had completed the background reading on Durkheim and was thinking about how to relate his ideas to adventure when I stumbled upon a connection while going for a run along the waterfront. From a distance I recognized the unusual profile of a style of boat that I had seen in sailing magazines. I jogged down the pier to look at the impressive 60-foot sailboat. Designed to be raced single-handed non-stop around the world, these boats are powerful, wide, lightweight racers. I was interested to find out that the boat was a Scottish entrant in the forthcoming 2012 Vendee Globe race (see www.vendeeglobe.org/en/). There was a website address written on the hull, and I was interested to read more about the boat, the race and the skipper. When reading the website – with Durkheim's concepts lurking in the back of my mind – I realized that this provided a good example of the way adventure can function to support and sustain social cohesion and social order.

Although there are many ways to analyse promotional material (e.g. critical discourse analysis, gender studies), my focus here is to consider how adventure and the adventurer are positioned to act as exemplars of a particular form of being Scottish. In particular, I'll illustrate how participation in this sailing event attempts to connect Scots, and people of Scottish ancestry, by appealing to values and norms that are both (supposedly) intrinsically Scots and inherent in adventure.

We can start by examining some text from the sailing team's website (Team Vendee Scotland, 2012). The 'Flying the flag for Scotland' page starts with lines from a Burns' poem where the poet proclaims 'My heart's in the highlands, wherever I go'. The author of the webpage claims that:

> these oft quoted lines from our national bard evoke that special sense of belonging that defines the true spirit of Scotland. This is the unique DNA that pulses through the veins of every native born Scot and lingers still in the hearts of an estimated 90 million descendants around the world, passionately protective of an enduring umbilical connection to the auld country which has been passed down from generation to generation. It is what brings us together as a family, united in pride of our heritage, history and culture.

This opening section is clearly aimed at connecting Scots and those of Scots descent (including this author) 'together as a family, united in pride'. One could obviously ask a number of questions that might disrupt this image. For example, is there a specific identifiable Scottish gene? Does the image of the highlands truly represent Scotland, where most of the population live in the lowlands of the south? And what of those of Scots descent who feel no pull to 'the auld country'? I realize that this website passage should not be read literally, but nonetheless it is appealing to a romantic notion that sustains heritage tourism in Scotland, and which promotes celebrations of Scottish culture in highland games and pipe bands in countries that are often geographically and culturally distant from Scotland (e.g. New Zealand and Australia).

The use of inclusive language, such as 'It is what brings us together', is a mechanism to define a social group to which one belongs by lineage rather than choice; Scots and their descendants are supposedly united and proud of their heritage, history and culture. This acts as a potentially powerful exercise in marking boundaries and excluding those who are not part of 'the club'. It is about creating an artificial sense of social cohesion.

The text continues:

> Intangible and indefinable, this is what distinguishes the Scots as a race apart – indomitable in the face of adversity yet forever generous of heart to others,

comfortable with who we are and the blessed privilege of being part of the greatest small country in the world. It has been said that if Scots were taken out of the world, it would surely fall apart.

I am sure that many other small countries would also claim that they exhibit many of these qualities that are apparently a distinguishing feature of the Scots (e.g. Danes, Norwegians or New Zealanders). The sailing team's intent, then, is to build an image of particular characteristics that are valued by Scots – to be strong in the face of adversity, to be generous to others, and to be self-assured.

The author goes on to cite a number of famous Scots, whose

> gifts to the world range from the telephone and television to penicillin, anaesthetic, radio, radar, colour photography, microwave ovens, the fountain pen, car tyres, raincoats . . . It runs in the blood too. Three quarters of all US Presidents have been of Scottish descent, as were the first men on the moon Neil Armstrong and Buzz Aldrin.

This image of Scots as key figures in history – as entrepreneurs, inventors, powerful politicians and adventurers – is designed to appeal to those who have been defined as part of the Scottish 'family' in the opening section of the website. Members of this family can be proud of who they are by vicariously basking in the achievements of their extended family. It is as if, simply through association with a Scottish entrant sailing around the world, people will come to possess the particularly Scottish qualities that the project espouses. Indeed, in the following passage we see the overt connection between the valued attributes of being Scottish and this particular sailing campaign:

> This legacy of adventure and achievement will no doubt be uppermost in the mind of John Mackay as he takes the helm of the aptly named *Spirit of Scotland* at the start of the Vendée Globe round the world race 2012.

Discussion

On the Team Vendee Scotland website, adventure and the adventurer are strongly linked to particular notions of Scottish identity. The website creates a sense of specific ways of being Scottish and portrays Scots as creative, tenacious and adventurous. As a 'Scot to his bones' it is natural, right and proper that John Mackay should be undertaking this adventure on a boat appropriately named the *Spirit of Scotland*. The website's rhetoric continues to valorize the white male adventurer embarking on a heroic solo journey, which is a common feature of the western adventure ethos. As Kane and Tucker (2007) have pointed out: 'The historic narrative of adventure has been centred on the heroic individual over-coming adversity . . . accounts of adventure are often viewed as inspiring and providing role models for society' (p. 30).

This project draws on various discourses as a means of promoting a sense of social cohesion (being Scots) and social order (the naturalness and desirability of adventure); indeed, there is a normative moral tone here about what it means to be a Scot. The website speaks from and to Scottish society's collective values. It serves as both the source and the guardian of (one version of) this society's values, which in this case sees adventure as something positive for all. This is supported by research that concluded that notable adventurers believed 'adventure was innovative, creative and vital to human existence itself' (Kane and Tucker, 2007, p. 37).

I suggest that adventure and adventurers in western society may be viewed as 'moral markers', as they reflect the shared values, norms and aspirations of the society from which they emerge. They are notable because they signify who we are, or who we might imagine ourselves to be, and they are rewarded for their adventurous exploits through sponsorship, media coverage and public recognition – all of which serve to reinforce the value of adventure to society. The adventurer is then revered because he/she embodies society's values and, through identifying with the adventurer (e.g. via sponsorship or social media), the public can 'participate' in the adventure.

If Durkheim was correct and modernity has altered the traditional sources of solidarity, then we are unlikely to find the moral certainty that he so earnestly sought in traditional structures of family and religion. However, despite the lack of these traditional social structures, society has not plunged into unmitigated chaos. Perhaps it is because the structures that Durkheim identified have not remained static but have changed with society, and because other social structures have emerged to fulfil a similar function. Perhaps, as Kane (2011) has pointed out, adventures provide 'a benchmark and guide to social knowledge and morals' (p. 1). This point was also made by Whitehead (1947), who suggested that adventure was a moral act insofar as it prevented the decay of civilization.

Society and individuals have shown themselves to be more adaptable than Durkheim gave them credit for. Adventure may function as one mutable element that has helped to sustain social cohesion and social solidarity in modern times, for, as Lynch and Moore (2004) have argued, adventure functions as 'both the current manifestation, and entrenchment, of an existing social and economic order and as a means of proving opportunities for new interpretations of personal and social reality' (p. 10). While I have suggested that adventure may play a role in social solidarity, it is by no means the only norm or value that might serve a bonding function within society.

Problematic aspects of Durkheim's theory

Durkheim's theory relating to the function that the collective consciousness plays has been developed into a branch of sociology referred to as *functionalism* or *structural-functionalism*. Durkheim's ideas had a huge influence on sociology in the twentieth century through the works of American sociologists Talcott Parsons and Robert Merton. As you will see in later chapters, however, functionalist approaches have fallen out of favour as other branches of social theory have been developed.

Durkheim's work has been principally criticized for maintaining the status quo. While he highlighted the importance of social consensus and social order, he downplayed the role of conflict (Giulianotti, 2005). Loy and Booth (2002) have argued that 'the most valid criticism of Durkheim's work is that conflict is notably absent from his theory of society' (p. 56). Durkheim's analogy of society as an organism, which existed in a state of equilibrium, failed to address issues relating to the unequal distribution of power and how a lack of conflict does not necessarily indicate that all members of a society are treated fairly. The lack of adequate theorizing about power has led Giulianotti (2005) to criticize Durkheim for failing to address how power inequalities operate to enforce consensus or conformity. Evidence of a social order does not necessarily equate to a just society. For example, some members of society may live in poverty or may be unable to vote, and are thus silenced.

Another criticism is that Durkheim failed to adequately account for the role of individual choice (agency) in the complex arrangements of social action. By emphasizing the collective consciousness as an objective reality, Durkheim promoted an overly deterministic interpretation of behaviour, which left little room for individual autonomy. Swingewood (2000, p. 78) explains that:

> One of the main problems with Durkheim's functionalism is that it eliminates the active role played by agents in the making of the various forms of social solidarity and patterns of social change. His approach ignores the question of how the moral values which hold society together are created and by whom.

While Durkheim may have erred by largely disregarding the role of the individual in maintaining social cohesion, he was not alone in struggling to solve this dilemma. The debate about the respective roles of 'external factors' (structures) and individual choice (agency) in determining action continues to fascinate us all. To denigrate Durkheim's overall contribution to sociology on the basis of the inadequacies of functionalism is overly harsh.

Conclusion

In order to fully appreciate Durkheim's influence, it is important to consider the cultural milieu that shaped his thinking and set his priorities. He has, for example, been criticized as a conservative thinker. Clearly this might be the case if he is contrasted with Marx, but this comparison is perhaps unfair. Indeed, while Durkheim did not take on Marx's revolutionary socialism, he 'was nevertheless a reforming liberal or socialist in political terms' (Craib, 1997, p. 14). Despite Durkheim's functionalism having been marginalized in many areas of sociological study, we are still dealing with the issues that confronted him: the relationship between society and the individual and how we might best deal with constant social change (e.g., globalization, new media, post-9/11 geo-politics). His writing contributed to an understanding of how society's values and norms are a 'reality' that influences individual actions. Adventure does not occur in a social vacuum; what is defined as an adventure and who are lauded as adventurers reflect a society's values.

Undoubtedly, Durkheim has left a lasting legacy, although this may not be apparent if one only reads modern texts. Indeed, fully appreciating contemporary social theory without an understanding of its foundations may not be possible. As Craib (1997) points out, Durkheim's theory continues to have value because 'there is such a thing as society and . . . there are various ways in which it imposes itself upon us; it is there and it works on us, whatever we might think about it' (p. 33). Durkheim's explanation for social cohesion may be found wanting, but his identification of a collective consciousness continues to have currency. Whenever we talk about social life, we invariably draw upon a set of values that comprise a collective consciousness. Adventure is one value that may function as a mechanism in achieving social cohesion. This cohesion may not 'stretch' across an entire society, but it may serve to bind sub-groups of like-minded people together (e.g. mountaineering or ocean racing communities).

In the discussion of adventure I used a critical perspective, based on a set of values and norms (an academic collective consciousness), to highlight how adventure might function in society. I have sought to draw your attention to the way that adventure can be used to support a society's collective consciousness. Appeals to adventure are loaded with meaning and serve to further particular interests and versions of society. The use of adventurous imagery to support particular versions of national identity is not unique to the Scots. For example, Kane (2011) has shown how Hillary's first ascent of Everest provided New Zealanders with an image that was aligned with 'a mythologised pioneering cultural identity' (p. 1). There is no 'natural' definition of adventure; it is socially constructed to serve particular purposes.

It is my hope that this chapter has encouraged you to think about adventure and adventurers in a new light. Whether or not adventure and adventurers will be successful in enhancing social cohesion into the future is another matter. If adventure is valued in society, then it might be possible for an adventurer to become a cultural hero. Whether John Mackay will be heralded as a 'true' adventurous Scot remains to be seen.

Adventure narratives provide a rich source of material for understanding the complexity of human nature and society for those willing to embark on a journey of enquiry. As a result of engaging with the material in this chapter, you should now be in a position to reflect on adventure and adventurers from a different perspective. As discussed, adventure is more than simply an individual act; it reflects and shapes the values and norms held by society.

Further reading

Of the references listed below, the texts by Jones (2003), Morrison (1995) and Swingewood (2000) provide useful introductions to Durkheim.

References

Craib, I. (1997) *Classical social theory*, Oxford: Oxford University Press.

Durkheim, E. (1893/1984) *The division of labour in society*, London: Macmillan

Durkheim, E. (1895/1938) *The rules of sociological method*, New York: Free Press.

Durkheim, E. (1897/1970) *Suicide: A study in sociology*, London: Routledge and Kegan Paul.

Durkheim, E. (1912/1995) *The elementary forms of the religious life*, New York: Free Press.

Giulianotti, R. (2005) *Sport: A critical sociology*, Cambridge: Polity Press.

Hughes, J., Martin, P. and Sharrock, W. (eds) (1995) *Understanding classical sociology: Marx, Weber, Durkheim*, London: Sage.

Jones, P. (2003) *Introducing social theory*, Cambridge: Polity Press.

Kane, M. (2011) 'New Zealand's transformed adventure: From hero myth to accessible tourism experience', *Leisure Studies*, DOI: 10.1080/02614367.2011.623305.

Kane, M. and Tucker, H. (2007) 'Sustaining adventure in New Zealand outdoor education: Perspectives from renowned New Zealand outdoor adventurers on the contested cultural understanding of adventure', *Australian Journal of Outdoor Education*, 11(2), 29–40.

Loy, J. and Booth, D. (2002) 'Emile Durkheim, structural functionalism and the sociology of sport', in J. Maguire and K. Young (eds), *Theory, sport and society* (pp. 41–62), Oxford: Elsevier Science.

Lynch, P. and Moore, K. (2004) 'Adventures in paradox', *Australian Journal of Outdoor Education*, 8(2), 3–12.

Morrison, K. (1995) *Marx, Durkheim, Weber: Formations of modern social thought*, London: Sage.

Swingewood, A. (2000) *A short history of sociological thought* (3rd edn), Basingstoke: Palgrave Macmillan.

Team Vendee Scotland (2012) *Flying the flag for Scotland*. Online: http://teamvendeescotland.com/flying-the-flag-for-scotland.html (accessed 27 September 2012).

Whitehead, A. (1947) *Adventures of ideas*, Cambridge: Cambridge University Press.

4

MAX WEBER

Rationalization and new realms of the commodity form

Peter Varley

the best things in life are not things

(Pine and Gilmore, 1999)

Introduction

This chapter explores the conditions of modernity as discussed in the writings of Max Weber, and considers how, in an age of advanced capitalism, adventure can be likened to a 'service product'. To this end, I will demonstrate how Weber showed that concepts of rationality, bureaucratization, control (regulation) and capitalist systems impact upon the life of the individual. I will then explain how these controlling influences allow for the containment and commodification of most aspects of human life, with particular attention to outdoor adventure and tourism. The specific example of the sea-kayaker is used throughout. This is because sea-kayakers currently occupy a curious place on the adventure commodification continuum (Varley, 2006), in that what they do is harder to turn into a totally controlled, risk-assured and predictable product than, for example, white water rafting or bungy jumping.

What follows is a short introduction to Max Weber the person and his academic biography. There is then a consideration of some key concepts developed in his work. These include the ideas that modernity is founded on the rationalization of society and natural phenomena; that the bureaucracy is in effect the organizational tool that underpins this rationalization; that time is measured and controlled in modern life; and that all of this may lead to experiences of disenchantment and a loss of spontaneity in our lives.

Background

Max Weber was born in Erfurt, Germany, in 1864 and lived through the biggest period of industrialization and social change in European history. He died in 1920. He grew up in an intellectually stimulating environment, in a family home where his father would regularly play host to well-known scholars and public figures of the day. Perhaps unsurprisingly, Weber was something of a prodigy and rapidly progressed to the universities of Heidelberg and eventually Berlin, where he gained his doctorate in 1889 and became a professor a few years later. He was a philosopher and sociologist who had a huge influence on the development of social theory and social research methods. Weber was a key instigator of *interpretivist* methodologies and presented sociology as a field that must study society through understanding the meanings that individuals attach to their own actions. He is regarded as one of the three key originators of modern social theory, the others being Karl Marx and Emile Durkheim. Weber's main intellectual concern was understanding the processes of rationalization, bureaucratization and resulting disenchantment that he associated with industrialization and the rise of capitalist society. In contrast with earlier ideas proposed by Marx, Weber suggested that the most important distinction between societies and individuals is not how people produce things, but how people think about each other and the world. His ideas have influenced a huge range of important thinkers in contemporary times, both in terms of new methodological approaches to social sciences and in understanding how society is structured and how social actors derive meaning from their experiences of it.

The root of his theorizing stemmed from a study of Protestant Ethics (1905/2001), in which a religiously promoted belief in a reward in the far-away distance (everlasting life) led to a way of living that valued the accumulation of material wealth and frugality. Thus, unostentatious wealth through hard work was considered a *sign* of the 'calling' from God, that one 'elected' to enter the Kingdom of Heaven and the state of grace. Unfortunately, of course, no one could really be sure what happens after death. From this uncertain torment, Weber argued, the spirit of modern capitalism was born. People were driven to accumulate capital, to invest and to work hard. It was in this sense that Weber argued that the ideals of *Protestantism* laid the foundations for the burgeoning of European capitalism and industrialization. I will now examine Weber's three principal concepts, rationalization, bureaucratization and control, and their relevance to an understanding of outdoor adventure.

Rationalization

The works of Max Weber highlight the changes in social life under the conditions of modernity. Weber saw *rationalization* as the systematic, measured application of science to work and everyday life. This idea of the application of rationalizing principles to industry is clearly illustrated in the fast-food industries, where time, product and experience are carefully controlled. Ritzer (2000), borrowing from

Weber's ideas, coined the term McDonaldization for these industrial processes brought to bear on everyday experiences (see also Chapter 13). Consider, for example, time, which in industrialized societies was rationalized into strictly controlled parcels: 20-minute tea-breaks, 50-minute school classes, 14 days' holiday and 39-hour work weeks. It is obvious how distinctly different capitalist, modern life is from that in traditional agrarian societies, where life was organized around natural cycles of day and night and the changing seasons.

The extension of rationality throughout all aspects of modern life produces a trend towards the elimination of emotion, spontaneity, randomness and surprise. This rather depressing vision of the unstoppable advance of bureaucratization and its imprisoning effects of precision, standardization and repetition (Rojek, 2000) may be the very conditions that spur the adventurers of late modernity to go out into the 'wilds' as a means of escape.

In *Economy and Society*, Weber (1922/1968) outlines four motives for social action: instrumentally-rational, value-rational, affectual and traditional (pp. 24–5). *Instrumentally-rational* motives for social action are determined by consistent and logical expectations of the behaviour of objects and of other human beings. These expectations are used as means for people to attain their own rationally calculated ends. Weber argued that instrumental rationality was the most important of the four motive types.

One example of this instrumental rationality in the world of outdoor adventure is the increasing focus on the measurement of skills and leadership abilities, via for example the British Canoe Union's (BCU) qualifications system. The logic is that rationalization of one's skills and leadership abilities can become the means to judge competence in the outdoors. This process can lead to a professionalization of adventure pursuits instruction, and a measurable system that allows formal judgements to be made about individual competence. This competence measurement is even given a numerical grade, so that a sea-kayak instructor may be level 4 or 5, or may be a 3★ leader for example.

Value-rational motives for social action are determined by the value one places on some ethical, aesthetic, religious or other form of behaviour – independent of its prospects for success. Value-rational motives influence actions for their own sake. For example, there is a growing 'leave no trace' ethic associated with leisure activities in wilderness areas. These values are adhered to by many kayakers, even though such behaviours may make the journey or expedition more difficult, as rubbish and human waste must be packed up and carried home rather than discarded or burnt.

Affectual motives are determined by a person's feelings and emotions. Weber (1922/1968) pays only fleeting attention to the sources of emotionally driven behaviour (aside from shame and guilt) and covers all other aspects of affectual motives with the catch-all phrase 'working off emotional tension' (p. 25). It is nevertheless clear that he was acutely aware of the influence of instrumental rationality as a suppressant of affective behaviour. This emotional tension is evident in the ways in which shame and guilt can become important aspects of the motives for the actions of contemporary adventurers. Consider how the anticipation of such emotions ensures that sea-kayak expeditioners take precautions to avoid falling foul of the instrumentally constructed 'rules of the game', such as leaving journey details and expected time of return with the coastguard. If adventurous action is ideally about coping on one's own in the face of risk and uncertainty, while also representing a form of escape attempt in the search for freedom, then adhering to 'rules' seems contradictory to many.

Traditional motives for social action are those derived from ingrained habituation. These are uncontested actions that come from convention and social norms, as in 'we've always done it this way'. Traditional motives are reinforced and maintained by habits and long-established behaviours. For example, the 'traditional' view is that experience is the great teacher in outdoor activities, and that booklets, courses and instruction manuals cannot adequately replace the time spent engaging in the activity. 'Time served' still garners respect in adventure activity circles such as those involved in sea-kayaking. Likewise, the ability to demonstrate a variety of rolls and perform self-rescues is often regarded as a basic requirement for more challenging paddles – but, of course, these are often not required.

It can be seen from these concepts of psychosocial motivation that a combination of instrumentally-rational and value-rational judgements determine much of what humans think and do, and that our emotions and traditions often play a less dominant role. In working life, for high social status to be arrived at, certain achievements are required. For example, success may be measured by an impressive rise through the hierarchical ranks in a person's place of employment. For sea-kayakers, long and exposed crossings, solo expeditions and island circumnavigations all bestow the achievers with admirable status among fellow participants and armchair adventurers alike. By the same token, being a BCU Level 5 paddling coach can confer rationalized, measurable status. As noted above, national governing body awards promote a 'rational' ladder of progression in the acquisition of technical skills and leadership and coaching abilities, as a method of objectively measuring an individual's competence in these areas.

Value-rational motives may assist with, or detract from, the urge to progress in the sea-kayaking world. If the individual expeditioner concerned holds time with her family as a core value, this may then cause conflict with her instrumental-rational values. If, conversely, she views her working or adventuring life as central to her ethical sense of self, the tensions may then evaporate, as she might argue that being a kayaker-expeditioner is as much a part of her as being a mother. In any case, Weber (1922/1968) would suggest that the problem tends to be approached rationally, rather than emotionally. Time may be carefully apportioned to each situation, and notions of 'quality time' with the family, as opposed to ordinary chore-filled, everyday time, might be set against 'play' time.

Far less easy to accommodate in modernity are the affectual and traditional motives. Perhaps the emotional ties with a sick and lonely relative, or critical comments from family elders about the demise of traditional motherhood, bring these motives into conflict with the instrumentally-rational ones, as they create incongruity and tension, which may lead to shame and guilt. It seems clear from Weber's work that affectual values are regarded as the least desirable for the promotion of capitalism in industrialized societies. Industrial societies require human performance to industrial standards, and emotions and affect must be managed out. Such qualities are an unwanted nuisance in an industrial society focused on efficient production (Ritzer, 2000).

Paradoxically, however, we may acknowledge the emergence of a service-based 'experience economy' and the sale of 'adventure holidays', which feature the intentional packaging of activities that will conveniently and reliably stimulate certain predictable emotional responses; the bungy jump and the ropes course, which mix intense fear and excitement in one short package, are good examples of this trend. This is surely a peculiar moment in the progress of modernity and capitalism and points towards what might now be termed the adventure 'industry' and, as such, deserves further consideration. We now turn to the second of Weber's concepts being discussed in this chapter: bureaucratization.

Bureaucratization

The bureaucracy is a model of rationalization, and the origins of the word come from the latin *bur* (the red colour of Roman desks) and *krato* (Greek for strength). The strength of a bureaucracy rests, Weber (1922/1968) argued, on the principles of hierarchy (a pyramid structure of importance and power), meritocracy (promotion in the hierarchy based on rationally measurable achievement), impersonality (everyone is replaceable) and continuity (the hierarchical structure can exist independently of the need for charismatic individuals and continues even when they leave). Weber, in his account of the bureaucracy, stresses impersonality; the allocation of functions, rule systems and the processes of documentation; and the notion that these machine-like structures will function irrespective of individual members and their characteristics. For Weber, this 'deadening' characteristic inherent in bureaucracies led to a *disenchantment* of human beings' relationships with the world and each other.

Bureaucracies behave in predictable ways and produce socio-structural stability and security, but they also affect the mentalities of those who inhabit them (Cashmore 1996): structured behaviour is expected and enforced through workplace discipline, norms and values; many social interactions are formalized as meetings, committees, interviews and appraisals; communications are recorded and filed for reference; and the constant surveillance of working life demands the 'inner modernization' of individuals in order for them to conform to these challenges (Becker, 1996). Thus, it might be argued that the propensity of some sea-kayaking enthusiasts to tick off the big circumnavigations or open crossings which they have managed may in some ways be a reflection of an *inner modernization*; these aesthetic experiences are reduced to a bureaucratic checklist.

Here again we see how, for Weber, calculability becomes an organizing principle in a person's overall personality. The continued dominance of traditional and value-rational behaviours by instrumentally-directed ones in modernity has restricted emotional responses in many aspects of social life. This has contributed to the dehumanization of social interactions, upon which cold, efficient bureaucratization is built (Sica, 2000, p. 52). Increased material comfort and rational control over one's life may be achieved in modern industrial society, but it is often at the expense of 'traditional features of closeness, flexibility and spontaneity which make life worth living' (Rojek, 2000, p. 9). Indeed, Weber (1922/1968) wrote of the 'unprecedented inner loneliness of the single individual' (p. 104) and the elimination of magic from the world. These are his descriptions of what he referred to as disenchantment, in which the bureaucracy is portrayed as a dehumanizing place in which to work, or in which to be a consumer; everything is predictable, and creativity and the unexpected are managed out. The adventure 'industries', such as activity centres and indoor facilities, are designed precisely to remove the uncertainty; in this regard, sea-kayaking tends to retain its natural, rich and less predictable form. Yet, paradoxically, sea-kayaking guides are expected to manufacture magic and excitement, to 'wow' their clients and give them a great time.

Regulation

The third of Weber's (1922/1968) big ideas that we are discussing is *regulation*. Regulation is closely related to rationalization and bureaucratization, and can be seen when controlling features of competitive sports are applied to hitherto freeform adventurous activities (e.g. kayak racing). Competitions of any sort have, by definition, to regulate behaviours in order to render them measurable. For example, it is accepted practice for sea-kayak races to have a long list of rules regarding personal competence, permitted boat types, timing, equipment required and rules regarding the route, with which all competitors must comply.

This general emphasis on control and predictability is further exemplified in a number of ways in adventure leisure markets; for example, there is the rapid growth in sea-kayaking outfitters along the world's coastlines. New kayakers are often required to undertake training courses in order to assure the safe operation of their equipment and sensible precautionary behaviour. Such courses inevitably become part of a process of self-disciplining and inner modernization, as the behaviours are expected and wrapped in a sense of social responsibility. Members will then learn to criticize and morally condemn those who go outdoors unprepared or without the right kit ('they were just kids – paddling 'round the skerries in an inflatable dinghy!').

Further regulation and control have emerged in the form of informal club rules that have become generalized, objectified and popularized through national governing bodies such as the British Canoe Union. The BCU publishes handbooks and instruction pamphlets, provides courses for the dissemination of skills and qualifications, and has copious written policies that are designed to govern members' behaviour. In this way, accepted, standardized views on ethical issues and certain practices are constrained by officially acknowledged, rather than informally agreed, skills and expertise.

It should now be clear that the advent of the bureaucracy and the encroachment of rationalization into everyday life allow the scarcest of resources to be carefully measured and managed: time. While adventures take place outdoors, where nature is superordinate, most of modern life is largely lived indoors, where industrial standards can more easily be applied, and unpredictable natural forces such as wind and rain kept out. I now turn to the role of *time* as an aspect of Weber's analysis of the progress of modernity.

Industrial time and play time

In spite of his acknowledgement of the importance of money to the modern individual, Weber (1905/2001) rejected the economic determinist views of those who, following Marx, would have it that all human actions are 'material' (economically motivated) in essence. He argued strongly that although economic interests were likely to motivate human action in some situations, there were far more complex issues that shape individual behaviour. Central to this in the Protestant Ethic was the pursuit of salvation through the disciplined spirit of hard work and enterprise, and from which all joy was absent (Hamilton, 2000). At this point, it may be useful to provide an outline of another tenet of Weber's puritan teachings: the appropriate use of one's time.

As the industrial era flourished, a modern view of how non-work time might be used was taking shape. As Rojek (1995) explains, leisure and work became divided into public and private spheres, and the pursuit of hard work and resistance to the temptations of idleness, pleasure, vanity and shallow enjoyment for its own sake was an illustration to others that you were chosen to enter heaven. In the classic quotation, Weber (quoted in Rojek, 1995, p. 46) states:

> Waste of time is the first and in principle the deadliest of sins . . . Loss of time through sociability, idle talk, luxury, even more sleep than is necessary for health . . . is worthy of absolute moral condemnation.

Things have changed. There is now a vast marketplace offering convenient packages of excitement, difference and adventure. 'Play' time is compressed and fitted around our working commitments, so that adventure centres must provide concentrated activity 'taster' weekends that maximize the adrenaline hits administered by qualified 'adventure professionals'. Chris Loynes (1996) identified the paradoxical trend for the 'control' of adventure in his article 'Adventure in a bun' (also see Chapter 13). He wrote about a company called 'Grippers', which is 'committed to offering participants the four biggest buzzes you can get in the area – guaranteed! Reliable products supposedly satisfy customers and are also amenable to audits to ensure "quality"' (p. 52).

The recent commercial success of bungy jumping is perhaps testimony to the viability in the market of the commodification of certain outdoor adventure experiences (see Chapter 3). In the quest for that beautiful, exciting moment, people spend considerable amounts of their disposable time- and money-budgets on ensuring that the desired emotions will be evoked (Becker, 1996). In many instances there's a controlled element of risk that we might call *adventure flavouring*, and a distillation of emotional experiences into a rationalized, repeatable package that is modelled according to market demand. The rationalizing processes of the bureaucratic mechanisms and regulatory systems that have emerged to support these adventure programmes in turn provide the predictability, risk reduction and control necessary for the processes of rationalization to invade more and more facets of social life.

Conclusions

This chapter began with an analysis of the ways in which the processes of rationalization, bureaucratization and regulation so necessary to modern capitalism pervade an ever-increasing proportion of our everyday lives. The provision of outdoor instructor schemes, the accepted practices and policies of national governing bodies and the widespread availability of reliable, replicable adventure experiences are suggested as natural extensions of Weber's three key ideas that I have discussed.

Readers might wish to consider how the rationalization processes of industrialization both enable a wider engagement with adventurous leisure possibilities and dilute or negate their desired effects. This 'dilution' may take the form of a nagging acknowledgement that one is dependent upon experts, rather than one's own ability, and a realization that the magic of the outdoors has been 'managed out'. People, individually or in small groups, embarking on adventures – and thereby deliberately putting themselves through hardships and dangers with minimal support – might be seen as responding to their disenchantment with life in the modern world. Undertaking an outdoor adventure, then, becomes viewed by many as both an attempt to escape from modernity's 'iron cage' and a quest for authenticity. The sea-kayakers, in particular, can be self-sufficient, bound by 'natural' rather than industrial time, and will have substantially less recourse to the safety nets of modern life as they pursue their leisure activity. If these possibilities become rationalized and controlled, opportunities for fulfilment, enchantment and the magic of adventure become harder to realize.

Further reading

There are two excellent papers listed below on the progress of rationalization in outdoor leisure. Both focus on climbing rather than sea-kayaking. There is also my own article (referenced below) on the commodification of adventure in general, of which rationalization and control are a necessary part.

Hardy, D. (2002, October) 'The McDonaldization of mountaineering: Conflicts between rock climbing culture and dominant value systems in society'. Paper presented at the International Conference on Outdoor Recreation and Education, Charleston, SC.

Heywood, I. (1994) 'Urgent dreams: Climbing, rationalisation and ambivalence', *Leisure Studies*, 13(3), 179–94.

Weber's work is largely contained in big volumes, with the main one being *The Protestant Ethic and the Spirit of Capitalism* (referenced below), where the most powerful passage for me is on pages 124–5; it's an eloquent commentary on the futility of materialism and the disenchanting effects of rationalization. Elster's work is also interesting, along similar lines:

Elster, J. (2000) 'Rationality, economy and society', in S. Turner (ed.), *The Cambridge companion to Weber* (pp. 21–41), Cambridge: Cambridge University Press.

References

Becker, P. (1996) 'In quest of paradise: Comments on the current attractions of excitement and adventure', *Journal of Adventure Education and Outdoor Leadership*, 13(2), 67–70.

Cashmore, E. (1996) *Making sense of sports*, London: Routledge.

Hamilton, A. (2000) 'Max Weber's Protestant Ethic', in S. Turner (ed.), *The Cambridge companion to Weber* (pp. 151–71), Cambridge: Cambridge University Press.

Loynes, C. (1996) 'Adventure in a bun', *Journal of Adventure Education and Outdoor Leadership*, 13(2), 52–7.

Pine, B.J. and Gilmore, J.H. (1999) *The experience economy: Work is theatre and every business is a stage*, Boston, MA: HBS Press.

Ritzer, G. (2000) *The McDonaldization of society*, London: Pine Forge Press.

Rojek, C. (1995) *Decentring leisure*, London: Sage.

Rojek, C. (2000) *Leisure and culture*, London: Macmillan Press.

Sica, A. (2000) 'Rationalisation and culture', in S. Turner (ed.), *The Cambridge companion to Weber* (pp. 42–58), Cambridge: Cambridge University Press.

Varley, P. (2006) 'Confecting adventure and playing with meaning: The adventure commodification continuum', *Journal of Sport and Tourism*, 11(2), 173–94.

Weber, M. (1905/2001) *The Protestant ethic and the spirit of capitalism,* London: Routledge.

Weber, M. (1922/1968) *Economy and society: An outline of interpretive sociology*, ed. G. Roth and C. Wittich, Los Angeles: University of California Press.

PART II

Modern social theorists
and adventure sports

5

ANTONIO GRAMSCI

Freestyle kayaking, hegemony, coercion and consent

Jerry Tracey

Introduction

This chapter will draw connections between freestyle kayaking and Antonio Gramsci, who was an Italian revolutionary and leading communist during the 1920s and 1930s. Although this connection may seem surprising, Gramsci's thought has been widely applied well beyond its original national and historical context. In particular, his development of the concept of *hegemony* has been widely drawn upon for the analysis of trans-national corporate business, and has been used to provide an explanation for the growth and dominance of global capitalism. Gramsci can also provide a useful framework for the interpretation of cultural interaction and social change. The evolution of freestyle kayaking will be used in this account as a means of illustrating this line of sociological thought.

It is likely that many readers will have experience of white-water sport and are therefore already familiar with the character of freestyle kayaking and the broader playboating subculture; for others, however, the following brief description may be helpful.

Freestyle has emerged relatively recently as an organized discipline of white-water kayaking from the 'new school' paddling culture of playboating. This form of activity has similarities to extreme sports such as windsurfing and snowboarding; like them, it is characterized by an expressive and individualistic style, within a highly sociable atmosphere in which display to other participants and spectators is a key element. At freestyle events contestants take turns to ride a large river wave or breaking hole in front of a panel of judges, who allocate scores based on the range and standard of the moves and tricks that are performed. As in surfing competitions, elimination takes place through a series of heats to create thrilling head-to-head final rounds.

Freestyle began originally with open contests known as 'white-water rodeos', but it has become progressively more structured over the years and there are now formal ranking systems that lead up to seriously contested places on national teams.

Nowadays, despite a continuing rhetoric of informality, many freestyle paddlers are visibly engaged in serious competition in officially recognized events. While early international championships were run on an *ad hoc* basis, they are now formally recognized by official governing bodies and have become integrated into the general sport–media–business complex. Meanwhile, the advent of this discipline appears to have stimulated a reverse change in the longer established forms of the sport, such as slalom, which has also become more spectacular in its displays of dramatic expression.

This chapter will use a Gramscian neo-Marxist framework to interpret these developmental changes within white-water paddlesport. The example of the evolution of sociable playboating into competitive freestyle will be used to illuminate the much broader issue of the intricate relationship between apparently resistant cultural forms and the real interests of American-led, trans-national business.

Background

You will have noticed the term 'neo-Marxist' in the above paragraph. As outlined in Chapter 2, Marx was largely responsible for two major concepts: the idea of evolutionary process in history and the interpretation of social structure as a mirror of economic relationships. In common with other major intellectual figures from the same period, such as Darwin and Freud, Marx did not create a fixed edifice but instead inaugurated a school of thought that later followers have greatly refined. Theorists who took Marx's concepts and built on them can be labelled neo-Marxists. Gramsci was one of these people.

Antonio Gramsci was born in 1891 and came from relatively humble origins on the Italian island of Sardinia. This background, and the struggles that his own family faced in reduced circumstances, gave him a deep sympathy with the Italian working class and a personal insight into the plight of the rural poor. A childhood accident left him with a hunchback deformity and permanently weakened health. However, through good educational progress and intellectual promise, the young Gramsci eventually made it to Turin University on the Italian mainland. There he became increasingly involved in left-wing politics during the turbulent period of the Great War and its aftermath. He emerged as a prominent socialist journalist, and in 1919 he became editor of the paper *L'Ordine Nuovo* (The New Order), which was a key mouthpiece for the revolutionary left.

Gramsci was personally involved in attempts to spark a Russian-style revolution in Italy, which was driven by a factory council movement (and the industrial workers it represented) in the northern cities. He was one of many at that time who believed that Italy was ripe for a proletarian uprising against a political system that had resulted in the carnage of the Great War. There was, indeed, a credible prospect of overthrowing the ruling elite, who had incompetently led the country into near disaster against Austria. Ultimately, however, these revolutionary initiatives failed. Subsequent to this setback, Gramsci spent an extended period of time in Moscow, where he met Julia Schucht, whom he married in 1922. Following his return to

Italy in 1924, he became the leader of the Italian Communist Party, at a time when the political left was coming under greatly increased threat from the rising forces of fascism.

As is well known, Mussolini seized absolute power and successfully established a fascist regime in Italy. Gramsci held technical immunity from arrest as a serving member of parliament, but he was nevertheless among those rounded up and imprisoned in 1926. Life in prison broke his already fragile health and he never regained his freedom. Near the end of his life Gramsci was transferred to a special clinic, but he died prematurely in 1937 while still under fascist custody.

Gramsci was far from idle during his long years in prison. In spite of his prolonged struggle with failing health, he undertook a major philosophical project. This extended Marxist thinking to provide an explanation for the clear persistence of capitalism in Western Europe and the absence or failure of the expected revolutions. Within a Marxist framework, he also accounted for the rise of fascism and the conspicuous support shown for it by some sections of Italian society – especially (and surprisingly) many members of the lower middle class and the peasantry. Central to Gramsci's explanations was the concept of *hegemony*, through which a ruling formation can use popular culture to engineer dominance by consent.

Following Gramsci's death, his extensive prison notebooks were retrieved by his sister-in-law and smuggled to Moscow, where they were safely stored by his wife's family until after the Second World War. Edited versions of his copious writings were finally published in Italian during the late 1940s, and in English and French translation during the early 1970s (Hoare and Smith, 1971). In the context of the Cold War, moderate communists in Western Europe found that Gramsci's sophisticated and evolved version of neo-Marxism provided a highly valuable counter-argument to the hard-line Stalinist doctrine that was emanating from the Soviet Union. It also offered these moderate communists a philosophical basis for a peaceful road to socialism by means of a gradual cultural transformation of society.

In addition, the Gramscian framework of analysis provided a pivotal theoretical background for the Centre for Contemporary Cultural Studies, which emerged during the 1970s and 1980s in Birmingham, England (Hebdige, 1979). Many cultural practices that were oppositional to capitalism were identified during these studies, and it was suggested that a strong tendency exists for these to become adopted by commercial interests and modified into forms that actually reinforce the existing social order. This line of interpretation of social life drew heavily on Marxism and on the concept of *hegemony* that had been developed by Gramsci. This idea is explained in the next section.

Key concepts

Hegemony

Gramsci's writing ranged over many areas and his prison notebooks are extensive and complex. The work was unfinished and includes rough notes on his thoughts that were probably not intended for an outside audience. In addition, he was obliged to use a code in order to mislead his prison guards and the fascist censors; Marxism, for instance, is referred to as 'the philosophy of praxis' and Lenin is called 'Illich'. However, his work included the development of a key concept with wider application: the idea of hegemony. Gramsci used this to account for the failure of revolution in Western Europe and to provide a Marxist explanation for the rise of fascism. The Gramscian idea of hegemony will be applied to a very different context here, since the concept will be illustrated through discussion of the relationship between the trans-national leisure business and the freestyle form of kayaking.

The evolution from informal and sociable playboating to the structured and codified discipline of freestyle can be seen as an instance of a path of development that has often been identified in other extreme or lifestyle sports. In general terms, this pattern starts with an alternative counter-cultural activity that is initially developed by pioneering practitioners. The new form of sports practice then becomes adopted and virtually taken over by commercial interests, which use it as a marketing tool and may promote it to a broader audience as the latest 'craze'. In time, a core of serious exponents emerges, whose spectacular exploits can threaten to undermine the image and status of an associated major sport. The response to this situation is a process of absorption, through which the alternative activity becomes re-invented as a new discipline within the established structures of formal sport. Examples of this process are provided by the integration of snowboarding into the structures of skiing, of windsurfing into those of sailing and of mountain-biking into those of cycling.

One possible theoretical lens through which this pattern of transformation can be interpreted is this concept of hegemony. It refers to a process in which a ruling group makes conspicuous concessions towards the demands of a resistant faction or rising class; due to this, the challenging formation appears to have achieved many of its objectives, but the actual result is a hybrid situation that in fact strongly favours the real interests of the dominant forces (see Jarvie and Maguire, 1994, pp. 108–29). In this way, a dominant group, such as Italy's inter-war fascists, can negotiate consent, or even approval, for its power from those whom it dominates. Gramsci was clear in his exposition of hegemony that it included an element of coercion. In addition to engineering widespread consent, the ruling group retains the option of using direct force against any remaining dissidents who fail to grasp the 'common sense' that there is no alternative to enthusiastic compliance. Under our present regime of global capitalism, people are not taken out and shot (at least not in the West), but firm sanctions are still applied against any who directly threaten the system or who stray beyond the boundaries of approved opposition.

In the case of freestyle kayaking, trans-national business interests made significant concessions to local canoe and kayak clubs and national administrative structures in order to gain their support for the promotion of playboating and its associated merchandise. However, the resulting emergence of freestyle as a formally organized discipline brought playboating culture into the mainstream, and opened the rest of the sport to much greater levels of media influence and commercial exploitation.

Despite initial appearances, the long-term profit goals of the global leisure industry were thus ultimately furthered by the pattern of development that occurred. There is, though, something of a paradox here; as in the case of other extreme forms of sport, many of the early pioneers of playboating were engaged in a direct protest against the social order in general, and the structures of sport in particular. Notwithstanding the later widespread commercialization of the activity and the advent of formal freestyle competition, echoes of this resistance remain visible in the culture of playboating today.

In a similar way to Gramsci's development of Marxism, his own work has itself been taken further and adapted to new circumstances. Two of these extensions to the Gramscian concept of hegemony are worthy of discussion here: Williams' (1977, 1982, 1983) analysis of the relationship between different forms of culture and Harvey's (2000, 2005a, 2005b) work on the power dynamics of trans-national business and global capitalism.

Dominant, residual and emergent cultures

Williams (1977, 1982, 1983) employed Gramsci's conceptual framework to investigate the interaction between high and popular forms of culture. In particular, he disputed the common Marxist view that leisure and culture are secondary to the world of productive work, as he saw popular culture as a key mechanism for the establishment and maintenance of ruling-class dominance by consent. Williams' version of hegemony has been characterized as 'hegemony lite', since he strongly emphasized the consent to domination that can be engineered through popular culture rather than through the underlying dimension of coercion. In the outdoor adventure context, examples of such a manufacture of consent can be seen in the diversion of the anti-establishment protest ethos of new activities, such as kite-surfing. This has recently undergone a familiar process that was seen before in snowboarding and mountain-biking, in which commercialization and the involvement of major business sponsors led to the introduction of formal rules and absorption into official structures of organization. Kite-surfing has now followed its predecessors down this route to gain the ultimate marker of mainstream social acceptance: the status of an Olympic sport. It will be interesting to observe those activities that still currently have a strong pioneering and alternative character, such as slack-lining, to see if a similar pattern of development occurs.

Williams (1977) produced a typology of cultural forms, which classed them as dominant, residual or emergent (pp. 121–7). The cultural practices of those in power are classed as *dominant forms*, together with activities that are directly promoted to the wider population through education, for instance. *Residual forms* are the persisting social interests of previously powerful or significant groups. Sometimes practices of this type can undergo spectacular revivals and re-emerge with a transformed nature. Finally, *emergent cultural forms* are those embraced by rising social groups. Such practices tend to be marginal at first but can herald styles of social interaction that are destined to become important in the future.

Emergent cultural practices can threaten to disrupt the established social order by providing a focus for opposition and challenge; the dominant formation, however, usually engages with any such new social behaviour and organizes 'diversionary channels' for it, such as structured programmes of approved events. This continuous process is seen as crucial to the maintenance of hegemony by the capitalist ruling class. Williams (1977), along with other neo-Marxists, regarded this ongoing upkeep of 'domination through consent' as a significant reason for the conspicuous absence of a social and economic revolution under contemporary corporate capitalism (p. 114). Like Gramsci himself, Williams (1982) believed that efforts should be made to counteract this ruling class hegemony through building alternative forms of culture among workers and their families (p. 40).

Within Williams' framework, our example of freestyle kayaking could be viewed as an instance of an emergent culture. Playboating expressed a clearly oppositional stance back in its early days. This was even the case within the sport; in the 1970s and 1980s informal playboaters were often seen as maverick intruders at regulated events, such as wildwater races. As is often the case with emergent forms, dominant business interests from the wider capitalist society adopted playboating as a new pursuit and began to actively promote a modified version of it as a marketing tool for leisure products. Commercial sponsors encouraged playboaters to embrace integration with the wider sport of kayaking and support its codification into the new structured discipline of freestyle. The new style of paddling rapidly transformed into simply one more branch of the dominant white-water sports culture, with the full support of the ruling establishment, which included the governing sports authorities. Following Williams (1982), this process could be interpreted as the taming of an emergent oppositional activity by dominant forces (pp. 40–2), as these businesses employed the adapted and controlled version of playboating to maintain and widen their ruling hegemony in the world of white-water kayaking.

Longer-established disciplines of kayaking, such as slalom, can be seen as residual forms of hegemony, since they date from an earlier period, when the values of amateur sport were dominant. A number of these older disciplines have undergone conspicuous revival in recent years, although their present regenerated forms have become highly dependent on the demands of commercial interests and the requirements of the media. In the case of slalom, especially, this visible change has been largely due to the influence of the emergent culture of freestyle, which has thus served to augment the hegemony of free-market capitalism. The needs of spectators have always been a central consideration in the organization of freestyle events, but slalom has tended to be much more geared around the enjoyment of actual participants. In recent years, however, there has been a strong trend towards much shorter and more intense slalom courses, which allow spectators to see most of the action from a single vantage point. In addition, championship level slalom has now mirrored freestyle by adopting a system of elimination through heats and semi-finals, in order to create dramatic final rounds that have greater appeal to the media and spectators.

Neo-liberalism and global capitalism

Gramsci wrote in the specific context of inter-war Europe. Unsurprisingly, his theoretical analysis was originally intended to address the particular situation of the failure of socialist revolution in Italy, and the appearance instead of a rising tide of fascist power. More recently, his explanation of the mechanisms by which capitalism can entrench its hold on society has been applied on a broader scale to the current situation of global interaction. Notable here is the work of Harvey (2000, 2005a, 2005b), who has used hegemony theory to outline a global trend towards dominance by vast trans-national corporations. Harvey suggests that the interests of these companies are increasingly backed by the advent of neo-liberal political systems, which are characterized by their support for an unrestrained free market, together with the widespread privatization of infrastructure and services. He points to the roles of Americanized forms of popular culture and mass media entertainment in maintaining this hegemony of American-led big business.

Freestyle kayaking could be viewed as contributing to this hegemonic process. Along with the other extreme forms of sport with a 'Californian cachet', it forms part of the ubiquitous and standardized American-style popular culture that is rapidly spreading across the globe in a process that Horne (2006) refers to as 'the production of consumption'. This refers to business interests influencing culture by creating artificial demands for consumer goods, from which they can subsequently profit from fulfilling. In the case of freestyle kayaking, sponsored 'pro-paddlers' regularly create elaborate new moves and tricks and exhibit them at high-profile events with extensive media coverage; it is almost invariably the case that these stunts can only be replicated by those who have purchased the very latest branded equipment!

Limitations and critiques

Gramsci made a major contribution to left-wing philosophy and these days he is normally associated with the idea of a gradual transition to socialism rather than turbulent upheaval. In view of this, it is perhaps rather disappointing to find that he was not, in fact, an advocate of peaceful protest and passive resistance in the Gandhian mould; it is clear that he was a strong supporter of armed insurrection in the 'right' circumstances, such as those faced by Lenin in Russia. We should remember, however, that Gramsci lived through very violent times and that his principal opponents, Mussolini's fascists, regularly had people tortured and shot.

Gramsci placed great emphasis on the importance of popular culture as a mechanism for the maintenance of ruling class dominance. He also stressed that those who hoped to achieve social change in developed societies needed to first develop and promote alternative and oppositional forms of culture. He had learnt from bitter personal experience that a direct assault on the power structures of the state could not work in Western Europe, despite its success in Russia. Nevertheless, Gramsci remained committed throughout to the fundamental Marxist concept that economic relationships are the base that determines the social structure of society. This general line of thinking has been widely challenged by those who attribute a much greater influence to individual free choice and who therefore ascribe a prime function to human agency. It can also be argued that ideas and original thought may have a much greater effect on human behaviour and on social development than Marxists, Gramscian or otherwise, are prepared to recognize.

Gramscian hegemony theory, along with structuralism and other forms of neo-Marxism, has been regarded by some of its post-modernist critics as a 'modernist grand narrative', which claims to offer an all-embracing interpretation of the dynamics of society (see Tosh, 2000, pp. 123–31). Wide-ranging theories of this type offer generalized explanatory frameworks that can help to generate under-standing of broad social and economic trends. They are not always very helpful, however, for the detailed study of the actual minutiae of everyday life. The realities of the social world are inevitably significantly more complex than a purely uncritical reading of any such broad macro perspectives or grand narratives would suggest. Therefore, social theories purporting to offer a total world-view, such as neo-Marxism and Gramscian hegemony, are probably best regarded as polemical starting points for thought and discussion rather than as definitive solutions.

Like other Marxists, Gramsci considered the primary division in society to be based on class. This was defined in terms of the relationship to the means of production, with workers being those who had to rely on the sale of their labour to the capitalist owners of machinery and materials. Later Gramscian analysts have pointed to the current dominance of a global business and finance class over a large general population of consumers (for example, Harvey, 2005a). While it provides a useful point of reference, this viewpoint is open to major criticism for seriously undervaluing other highly significant lines of social cleavage, especially those based on gender, ethnicity or religion.

Certainly, social commentators adopting a post-modern analysis often believe that we have moved far beyond the era of mass labour in heavy industry and into a post-industrial period of fluid relationships, transient identities, instant information flow and a multi-choice cultural menu. An alternative to hegemony theory, with this perspective, is provided by the work of Castells (2004). He analyses the role of freely chosen cultural practices as a means of asserting one's social identity within this contemporary 'network society'. It is becoming increasingly common in the Western world for the social character and status of people to be defined by their leisure and lifestyle choices, rather than purely by their paid occupation and their position in formal hierarchies. Castells (2004) argues that the availability of such flexible social options has become widened by the significant development of information and communication technology and its application to everyday life.

In addition, Gramscian hegemony theory has inevitably come under strong criticism from neo-conservatives, who favour Thatcherism and Reaganomics. They point to the success of capitalism in promoting efficient production and in spreading material prosperity in areas where it has been enthusiastically adopted, such as the 'tiger economies' of the Pacific Rim. Those who take this stance often suggest that overall human happiness and material well-being have greatly increased since the fall of the Soviet Union and the spread across the world of free-market economics combined with liberal-democratic politics (Fukuyama, 1992). These claims have, of course, been tempered by those who highlight catastrophic environmental damage and widespread exploitation of vulnerable people as consequences of this prosperity – especially in less-developed parts of the world (Klein, 2005).

Returning to our example of changes in white-water kayaking practice, there have indeed been some positive aspects to the commercial penetration of the sport, the emergence of which was greatly assisted by the advent of freestyle. For example, there have been conspicuous developments in the design and construction of boats and paddles that would have been unlikely without the driving motivation of business. Safety equipment and protective clothing have also been improved. The increase in numbers generated by media promotion has put some venues under strain, but has also led to the development of new purpose-built facilities.

Conclusion

This chapter has discussed one strand of the extensive development of Marxist thought beyond the influential (but flawed) basic version that was promoted by Soviet propaganda. In particular, Gramsci's concept of hegemony has been introduced and explained as the process by which dominance can be established through using popular culture to engineer consent. I hope that the issues raised will stimulate discussion and the sharing of opinions. This will in itself help us to more deeply question the widespread 'common-sense' view that there are no possible alternatives to the established capitalist system within which most of us live.

In common with other forms of Marxist theory, the Gramscian approach to social analysis can appear to be very negative. When seen from this perspective, society can seem riddled with conflict – with further class confrontation not only necessary, but inevitable. However, the fact that we have developed an awareness of our submission to the global capitalist system does not necessarily preclude us from enjoying its products.

Like other forms of Americanized popular culture, extreme sports are highly seductive. In the case of our example, freestyle kayaking is undeniably dramatic for spectators and thrilling for participants. Those of us who are addicted to surfing waves and playing rapids in commercially produced, plastic playboats can still find the activity liberating and uplifting on the personal level – even after becoming aware of our own exploitation. On the other hand, is this in itself an instance of the construction of hegemony, in which we are manipulated into giving consent to our own domination?

Further reading

Gramsci's own writing can be quite hard to follow, owing to its non-sequential thematic nature and his efforts to mislead the prison censors. However, the Hoare and Smith translation (referenced below) includes a full introduction and useful commentary notes throughout. A more concise anthology is available, which also includes extracts from Gramsci's journalism and early work:

Forgacs, D. (ed.) (1988) *A Gramsci reader: Selected writings 1916–1935*, London: Lawrence and Wishart.

Those interested in finding out more about the story of Gramsci's life and the context of his work should find this definitive historical study by Clark to be interesting and accessible:

Clark, M. (1977) *Antonio Gramsci and the revolution that failed*, London: Yale University Press.

An extensive secondary literature exists on Gramsci's political thought and philosophy. An example that is enjoyable to read is the analysis by Femia, which also includes a discussion of the later application of Gramsci's ideas:

Femia, J.V. (1981) *Gramsci's political thought: Hegemony, consciousness and the revolutionary process*, Oxford: Clarendon Press.

An example of the application of Gramscian thinking to the study of sport and leisure is provided by the work of Bairner. A good introduction is the following book chapter:

Bairner, A. (2009) 'Re-appropriating Gramsci: Marxism, hegemony and sport', in B. Carrington and I. McDonald (eds), *Marxism, cultural studies and sport* (pp. 195–212), London: Routledge.

References

Castells, M. (2004) *The power of identity*, Oxford: Blackwell.

Fukuyama, F. (1992) *The end of history and the last man*, London: Penguin.

Harvey, D. (2000) *Spaces of hope*, Edinburgh: Edinburgh University Press.

Harvey, D. (2005a) *A brief history of neoliberalism*, Oxford: Oxford University Press.

Harvey, D. (2005b) *The new imperialism*, Oxford: Oxford University Press.

Hebdige, D. (1979) *Subculture: The meaning of style*, London: Methuen.

Hoare, Q. and Smith, G.N. (eds) (1971) *Selections from the prison notebooks of Antonio Gramsci*, London: Lawrence and Wishart.

Horne, J. (2006) *Sport in consumer culture*, Basingstoke: Palgrave Macmillan.

Jarvie, G. and Maguire, J. (1994) *Sport and leisure in social thought*, London: Routledge.

Klein, N. (2005) *No logo*, London: Harper Perennial.

Tosh, J. (2000) *The pursuit of history: Aims, methods and new directions in the study of modern history*, Harlow: Longman.

Williams, R. (1977) *Marxism and literature*, Oxford: Oxford University Press.

Williams, R. (1982) *Problems in materialism and culture*, London: Verso.

Williams, R. (1983) *Towards 2000*, London: Hogarth Press.

6

NORBERT ELIAS

The quest for excitement in Parkour

Michael Atkinson

This chapter addresses key sociological concepts developed through the research and writing of German sociologist Norbert Elias. While often overlooked as a significant modern theorist, Elias's work not only pre-dated and predicted, but also drew together and synthesized, such major theoretical streams from twentieth-century sociology as social constructionism, structuration, dramaturgy, actor networks, co-evolutionary models, biopower, habitus and discourse analytics. In this chapter, I focus on two central concepts in Eliasian sociology, *civilizing processes* and *mimesis*, as a vehicle for unpacking and understanding the applicability of *figurational sociology* to the study of Parkour in Canada.

Norbert Elias and figurational sociology

Norbert Elias's figurational sociology rests between an academic rock and a hard place. His work was not discovered *en masse* by European or North American sociologists until the 1970s. By this time, many of Elias's themes, ideas, concepts and theoretical strands had already been 'discovered' by contemporary sociologists, social psychologists, philosophers or historians. Elias completed the main structure of his magnum opus, *The Civilizing Process*, in 1939 (a book setting the tone for his take on body research within the social sciences), but it would not be widely received until its (re)print in English in 1978.

Elias was born in Breslau on 22 June 1897, the only son of Hermann and Sophie Elias. At the distinguished Johannes secondary school in Breslau he received a first-class education in science, mathematics, classics, languages and literature. On leaving school in 1916 he served in the German military, mainly on the Western Front, during the First World War. He later enrolled at Breslau University in both philosophy and medicine, and completed the pre-clinical part of his medical training before concentrating on philosophy for his doctorate.

Shortly after receiving his degree in 1924, Elias travelled to Frankfurt, where he worked as an academic assistant in sociology, until he fled Germany in 1933, following the National Socialists' accession to power. Elias, as a Jew, went into exile in Paris for two years and eventually moved to London in 1935. In both Paris and London, Elias worked on *Über den Prozess der Zivilisation* [*The Civilizing Process*], which was published in 1939. Without an academic position, and therefore an academic audience for his work, his thoughts regarding bodies, societies and historical processes remained in relative obscurity. Elias would not obtain his first university post in sociology until 1954, at the University of Leicester in the United Kingdom.

Elias is likely best known for his analysis of social *figurations*; in many ways, this is his chief conceptual offering to sociology. Elias describes a figuration as 'a complex web of social relationships based on individual and group interdependencies, such as a family, a school, a workplace, a community, an economy or a political sphere' (Elias, 1978a, p. 208). He used the term 'figurations' instead of traditional concepts such as society, institution, subculture and other words that mean human action as being statically structured rather than ongoing every day. Elias (1978b, p. 214) further suggested that individuals' activities are best understood as products of mutual (but not necessarily equal) relationships:

> The network of interdependencies among human beings is what binds them together. Such interdependencies are the nexus of what is called the figuration, a structure of mutually oriented and dependent people. Since people are more or less dependent on each other, first by nature and then by social learning, through education, socialisation, and socially generated reciprocal needs, they exist, one might venture to say, only as pluralities, only in figurations.

The above description of a figuration is well worn within Eliasian-inspired research; indeed, this small excerpt contains several concepts that underpin his thinking about society. While Elias eventually published over a dozen books and a great many original articles and chapters articulating the merits of figurational analysis, his thought remains, to this day, almost exclusively referenced for his insight on manners, emotional restraints and the social control of violence. Although Elias's theoretical insights outlined in *The Civilizing Process* are applicable to the widest range of sociological subdisciplines, figurational theory is perhaps most consistently applied and debated within the sociology of sport (Dunning, 1999; Atkinson and Young, 2008). To this end, the application of figurational sociology to an alternative physical/adventure culture such as Parkour makes analytic sense.

The sociogenesis of the Parkour figuration

From the outset, Elias would encourage anyone studying Parkour (or *traceurs* – the term for those practising Parkour) to see the group as an historically developing network or web of interdependent actors. In a nutshell, this is the essence of figurational sociology. Ties may be strong in local Parkour 'crews', wherein members come to develop bonds, share activities, develop identities as traceurs, learn particular Parkour ideologies and perspectives, and become committed to Parkour. However, Elias would encourage students to think more broadly about Parkour as a social group spanning time and geographic space. Even though enthusiasts may not see themselves as tied to different Parkour scenes, groups, factions and social 'happenings' around the globe, they are nonetheless part of a global network of people who are actively shaping (and being shaped by) Parkour culture(s). Further still, Elias would, perhaps first and foremost, encourage us to see Parkour itself as a figuration developing in particular historical times, contexts and specific geographic spaces. To put it simply, Parkour does not simply emerge out of the social dust accidentally.

Let's begin to think about Parkour like a figurational sociologist. The physical cultural roots of Parkour date back over 100 years. What is now commonly known as Parkour or *free running* is a particular offshoot of a style of woodland training called *Hébertism*. Hébertism emerged in the early twentieth century through the athletic philosophies of French naval officer George Hébert. A lifelong advocate of intense physical training as a means of developing personal virtue, Hébert was particularly impressed by the physical development and body-environmental oneness of the indigenous peoples he encountered across the African continent. Hébert came to believe that the pursuit of physical perfection and communion with one's local surroundings is a technique for developing one's sense of place in the physical and social environment, and can be an effective vehicle for bringing forth the underlying essence of one's own humanity (Atkinson, 2009).

Upon his return to France in 1903, Hébert tutored at the College of Rheims, where he innovated a path-breaking physical cultural lifestyle. He designed a series of apparatuses and exercises to teach what he dubbed the *Natural Method* of physical disciplining. Hébert's Natural Method placed practitioners in a remote wooded setting, wherein they would be instructed to run from five to ten kilometres. Practitioners were simply told to run through the woods, over bushes, through streams, climb up and down trees, and traverse fields towards a pre-established destination. Students were also instructed, at particular time or distance points, to lift fallen logs, carry and throw heavy stones or even hang from trees. Hébert believed that, by challenging his students to practise basic human muscular-skeletal movements in uncontrolled settings, they would develop qualities of strength and speed towards being able to walk, run, jump, climb, balance, throw, lift, defend oneself and swim in practically any geographic landscape. Hébert felt that Natural Method practitioners would progressively learn to encounter and control any emotions or social situations they encountered in life. The Natural Method demanded that one possess sufficient energy, will-power, courage, coolness and *fermeté* (overall 'hardness' and strength) to conquer any physical or mental obstacle. In a moral sense, by experiencing a variety of psycho-emotional states (e.g. fear, doubt, anxiety, aggression, resolve, courage and exhaustion) during training, one cultivated a self-assurance that would lead to inner peace.

Hébert became the earliest proponent of what the French would later call the *parcours* (obstacle course) method of physical training. Modern woodland challenge courses and adventure races – comprising balance beams, ladders, rope swings and obstacles – are often described as Hébertism courses in both Europe and North America. It is even possible to trace a full array of modern children's playground equipment to Hébert's original *parcours* designs of the early 1900s. The contemporary, Anglicized subculture moniker 'Parkour' clearly derives from Hébert's use of the term *parcours(e)* and the French military term *parcours du combattant*. Indeed, Hébert's Natural Method of training had a special impact on French military training in the 1960s. French soldiers during the Vietnam War were especially inspired by Hébert's method and philosophy of physical and emotional development, and employed the Natural Method as a technique for honing their jungle-warfare skills. Among the French soldiers exposed to the Natural Method was Raymond Belle. Belle became proficient in *parcours* training methods and promoted their virtues almost as passionately as Hébert.

The crucial point here is that, following his tour of duty in Vietnam, Belle taught his son David the principles of the Natural Method. The younger Belle had participated in martial arts and gymnastics as a young teen and immediately took to the method. After moving to the Parisian suburb of Lisses, David Belle further explored the rigours and benefits of the Natural Method with his friend Sébastien Foucan. By the age of fifteen, Belle and Foucan had developed their own urban style of the Natural Method, which they termed Parkour. In a sense, their use of concrete and steel city spaces meshed well with Hébert's philosophy of immersing oneself in one's immediate physical/natural environment to gain a deep and personal awareness of it. In the 2003 BBC documentary *Jump London*, Foucan described his initial construction of Parkour as a physical and spiritual lifestyle of movement in which 'the whole town [Lisses] was there for us – there for free running. You just have to look and you just have to think like children. This is the vision of Parkour.'

Belle and Foucan gathered recruits and followers in Paris and then across Europe through the 1990s. By the end of the decade, Parkour had spread all over the world and included core groups in the United Kingdom, France, the Netherlands, Sweden, Australia, the United States and Canada (Wheaton, 2012). Since the early 2000s, the Parkour scene has diversified considerably, evolving into a global community comprised of various factions, such as Natural Method traditionalists, suburban and urban Parkour crews and, now, enthusiasts who push for the 'sportization' of Parkour (that is, the creation of international Parkour federations, training systems and competitions). Additionally, traceurs have been featured in television commercials, video games and movies. Major athletic brands have designed and sold Parkour running shoes and shorts, and Parkour-style fitness classes are cropping up in health clubs in North America.

This brief overview of the sociogenesis (or 'social development') of Parkour over the past thirty years illustrates another fundamental principle in figurational sociology: that much of what happens historically does so in interdependent but relatively *unplanned and unanticipated ways*. At no time, our best historical records indicate, did Hébert intend to design a physical cultural lifestyle that would develop into the global Parkour culture we see today, and nor did Belle or Foucan. Elias regularly described modern-day conditions as the unintended outcomes of long-term historical processes (1978a, 1978b). What is the significance of such a recognition? Well, primarily, it draws attention to the importance of understanding phenomena from a long-term historical perspective. Second, and perhaps more importantly, it pushes us to see events such as the development of Parkour cultures around the world as deeply tied to, and interdependent with, broad-scale social trends and events. And to be sure, Elias helps us appreciate that no physical culture like Parkour is divorced from the social structures, trends and events that shape our societies on a broad scale. Just think, if Hébert's Natural Method had not been a direct response to the 'softening' of (male) bodies as a result of Western industrialism, the burgeoning middle-class, sedentary lifestyles and what he called 'remedial' forms of physical education in schools, would there have been a Parkour? If Belle and Foucan had not experienced a sort of urban discontent, would a Parkour video game have become a part of popular culture?

In the remainder of this chapter, I explore the utility of Norbert Elias's work for deciphering the meaning of Parkour to a group of Natural Method enthusiasts in southern Ontario, Canada. These practitioners use woodland spaces in the area to practise as Hébert originally outlined. While this group does not, by any means, represent the ideologies, practices and ethics of all traceurs (or even a majority) in the global Parkour figuration, it provides an interesting case nevertheless.

Parkour and civilizing processes

Elias's figurational sociology places a firm interest in studying *social processes*. To an Eliasian-inspired sociologist, all aspects of social life are processual (meaning 'ongoing') by nature. Elias's emphasis on the primacy of attending to process in sociological analysis is captured by Goudsblom (1977, p. 105), who argued that Elias believed:

1 that sociology is about *people in the plural* – human beings who are interdependent with each other in a variety of ways, and whose lives [including their bodies] evolve in and are significantly shaped by the social figurations they form together. From the beginning, then, we cannot view traceurs as isolated individuals, but rather as part of a larger web of interconnected people sharing particular (though not necessarily identical) tastes and preferences for a social practice;

2 that these figurations are continually in flux, undergoing changes of many kinds – some rapid and ephemeral, others slower but perhaps more lasting. We cannot view, for example, the global traceur figuration as a static group, but rather as a constantly evolving social amalgam comprised of diverse actors with varied perspectives on the practice. Some of the ways in which Parkour changes as a practice come from within the group, while

others are a result of long-term, ubiquitous socio-cultural forces (e.g. market capitalism, globalisation, the mass mediation of society);

3 that the long-term developments taking place in human figurations have been, and continue to be, largely unplanned and unforeseen. In this case, no one plans out or maps the long-term development of Parkour culture. Instead, the global figuration develops in relatively unscripted manners; and,

4 that the development of human knowledge takes place within human figurations. Here, we might first stop to consider how people learn to become traceurs only in groups. Acquiring the skills and knowledge to be a traceur is primarily a group-based phenomenon.

Elias's emphasis on groups, processes and knowledge development underscores the need to think socio-logically about any phenomenon under study. When I first started interacting with a local Parkour crew of about twenty traceurs in Hamilton, Ontario, it became very tempting to focus on the activities, practices and perspectives of two people I became close friends with in the group during the ethnography: Trent and David. When conducting ethnography, and immersing oneself in the culture under study, it seems natural to study particular people in incredibly minute detail, and to become enraptured with their lives. But to think socio-logically about the traceurs' penchants for Parkour, I needed to see them as people living in Hamilton during a specific space in a time period categorized by particular socio-economic, political, ideological and material conditions.

Like the others in the group, Trent and David were lower-middle class and underemployed, were not driven to achieve academically in their youth, displayed preferences for hyper-masculine forms of risk-taking, were socially and politically conscious but relatively resistant to mainstream conservative ideologies, and had little background in organized sport. They were all born and raised in the downtown or east end of Hamilton, which is a city rife with social inequality and pervasive alternative youth subcultural scenes. Almost immediately, I began to see Parkour in Hamilton (practised in the woodlands of the west end) as an 'east ender' solution to the boring routines of everyday life.

Trent told me that Parkour means something to many of the young men he knows between the ages of thirteen and twenty-five because it provides them with a collective solution to similar problems of social exclusion and personal boredom. Hamilton is, by no means, a city on the cultural or economic move. It is a depressed economic space with an eroding downtown core. A quick city bus ride to the west end can provide members of the group with a free and accessible space to create a physical cultural community that takes them out of the socio-economic trappings of their everyday lives.

Let's return to Elias, who is globally recognized for his description of the *civilizing process* (1978a), which receives as much praise as it does criticism. Elias's analytic construction of the civilizing process is relatively straightforward, but complex and brilliant along many lines. In its simplest terms, the civilizing process refers to the degree to which, over many centuries (roughly the thirteenth century to the nine-teenth century), the evolving social organization of Western nations such as France, Germany and the United Kingdom influenced people in these nations to become more self-restrained in their personal and cultural practices. Elias argues that as these nations became increasingly dense in terms of their respective social divisions of labour, and the corresponding interdependencies shared by people therein widened, social thought and collective psychologies leaned more heavily towards *self-control*. The long-term development and spread of complex manners systems (including how to eat at the dinner table, how to dress modestly, how to manage one's natural body functions, and what constitutes appropriate sexual conduct) across these Western nations illustrated, to Elias, how the mantra of personal restraint and control domi-nated social life. This cultural shift in thinking and personal practice occurred and was arguably facilitated within emerging nations headed by central ruling authorities that 'owned' the legitimate means of violence and economic taxation. Elias (1978a) describes these structural and social transformations, combined with what he termed 'the parliamentarization of conflict', as unintended sociogenic changes. Here is where Elias's interest in many of the classic sociological questions (such as the nature of social organization, the relationship between the individual and society and how social change occurs) is revealed. Elias studied the body, in particular, as a marker of all these social processes, namely the process of social and then internal, personal self-regulation reflective of shifting social interdependencies between people.

How does this apply to the study of Parkour? The theoretical punch underlining Elias's description of civilizing processes is that personal self-restraint became the dominant psychological structure in the typical person's mindset, and I think this idea applies well to the study of traceurs. For example, my friends Trent and David have a lot to complain about in their lives. Neither grew up in the best of social environments; they had few material resources in their young lives and were not particularly supported in school. Rather than lashing out at people in everyday life, abusing their bodies with drugs and alcohol or engaging in other fatalistic pastimes, they, like so many other youth sport subcultures in North America (e.g. skate-boarders, BMXers, trials riders), develop physical cultural pastimes that allow them to manage and embody a sense of personal empowerment while expressing a *restrained* form of disenfranchisement. The act of going to the woods in order to do 'self-work' through Parkour is indeed a highly restrained form of social protest – a protest against their own sense of disconnection with broader society as young people on the socio-political margins, and against the ways in which their bodies are contained in everyday life in urban settings that do not allow for much free movement.

While it is beyond the scope of this chapter to illustrate the full thrust of Elias's notion of civilizing processes on Parkour, what is clear is that the sociogenesis of the practice might be tied deeply to broad-scale, city-wide social shifts. Elias's figurational sensibility teaches me to see the development and practice of Parkour as systematically tied both to the structural organization of nations and to trends in the collective psychological development of people in particular contexts and spaces.

Mimesis

Perhaps one of the most globally tapped concepts from Elias's work on sport and physical culture is that of *mimesis*. As we have seen, a central principle in figurational research on long-term civilizing processes is that Western societies have become relatively unexciting social environments. With the general pacification of cultures that occurs over time, a collective need to devise and institutionalize cultural activities that strike a balance between personal pleasure and restraint arises. As outward displays of emotion are pushed behind the scenes of social life in so-called civilized spaces (Elias 1978a, 1978b), individuals pursue a full range of activities that elicit excitement in highly controlled contexts of interaction (Maguire, 1993). So, figurational sociologists regularly examine the role of risk-based physical activities in arousing particular emotions that are regularly controlled in other spheres of life (see, for example, Elias and Dunning, 1986; Dunning, 1999; Atkinson and Young, 2008).

Both Trent and David spent a great deal of time with me articulating the less than exciting nature of their lives. Like so many of us, they get up early, go to work, spend long hours being 'pleasant' with customers (Trent is a mechanic and David is a personal trainer), go home for dinner, perhaps watch a bit of television or go for a drink with friends before heading off to bed. The next day, and the next and the next are virtually identical to the previous ones. Activities like Parkour, and this is true of so many leisure activities, disrupt the monotony of their lives. Why? Quite simply, because jumping and running in the woodland setting presents them with a series of self-directed physical and psychological risks. Hurling their bodies Parkour-style creates an emotionally rewarding balance between fear and pleasure. They are able to take physical risks and perform a kind of self-directed suffering they find enjoyable. As Trent told me one day, Parkour (in its Natural Method roots) is a balance between throwing yourself into the woods to see what you become and maintaining focus, control and an attitude of self-responsibility through the practice. You push and test yourself, he explained, but in such a manner that you maintain a sense of respect for others there, and the natural setting itself.

Let's run through (a bad pun) a typical Natural Method session. The guys in the Hamilton crew show up either after work or at the weekend for a thirty to ninety minute 'jam' (their term for a session). They know the lattice-work of trails running through west Hamilton well and will start by picking a point on the map (say four or five kilometres from one of the main trail access entry points). Their goal is to get to the pre-designated point in one straight line. If there is a river, cross it directly. If there are hills littered with boulders, climb them. This is not a race, per se, but a chance for the traceurs to learn the physical skills (they argue the skills of animals) required to move quickly, efficiently and often dare-devilishly through the course and then back again. At times, they construct the jam as a tribe moving towards a point of 'attack'. They might fall, become lacerated, get muddy or wet, or experience extreme exhaustion. This, they say, is fun.

Elias and Dunning (1986) argue that physical cultural games involving a moderate degree of self-directed pain and risk are generally tolerable and allow individuals to participate either as competitors or as spectators in behaviours that are taboo in other social spheres. In the words of figurational sociologists, Parkour facilitates a *controlled decontrolling of emotional controls* (Elias and Dunning, 1986). Simply put, participating in adventurous activities allows people to engage in risk-related activities, which permit them to act in the exact opposite ways to which they are 'supposed' to behave in almost all other spheres of life. Figurationalists call the sort of aggressive risk-taking showcased in sport-related physical cultures as *mimetic*, which means that while pain, suffering and injury often result for people who engage in risk-related sports, this sort of risk and self-aggression is often perceived as make-believe, since it is quasi-controlled by social norms and unwritten rules.

But why is there a need for mimetic social behaviours at all? A central idea in Elias's (1978) writings on long-term civilizing processes is that Western societies are now rather unexciting places. As standards of civilized, restrained and mannered behaviour are considered within middle-class spheres as 'normal', high levels of behavioural control become a learned 'second nature' for individuals. Within this context of containment, organized cultures emerge as a means for people to partici-pate in, or observe, that which is emotionally, psychologically and physically arousing. Even children's games like tag, Red Rover or hide-and-seek are playful expressions of hunting, chasing, battling and conquering pastimes that humans find thrilling.

Elias and Dunning (1986) suggest that one of sport/leisure/physical culture's primary roles within complex figurations is to de-routinize the emotional and psychological drudgery of our restrained, civilized lives. For the participants in adventure or risk-based physical cultures like Parkour, a session in the woods can provide a temporary liberation from the conservative, middle-class social codes that limit their physical, risk-taking affective outbursts. To this end, suggests Maguire (1993), athletic pastimes and cultures become socially revered as they establish contexts of *exciting significance* for participants.

Critiques

Like any other theoretical framework in the social sciences, figurational sociology has its limitations. Among the most significant of these shortcomings is that figurational sociologists seem to be able to reconcile anything being researched as an outcome or product of long-term civilizing processes. Rarely are figurational sociologists able to test or scrutinize the accuracy and legitimacy of this grand theory. Critics have charged figurational sociologists (most notably in sport studies) with treating the central aspects of Elias's work as accepted theory without seeking to amend, recast or reject elements of figurational sociological that do not hold up under empirical analysis. Elias himself argued that figurational sociology should not be approached as a total and completely perfect theoretical system, but rather as a set of 'sensitizing' principles and ideas for thinking socio-logically.

A second critique, and what is especially frustrating, disappointing and curious about Elias's reception in Western sociological circles, is the collective overemphasis on 'matters civilizing' in his work. The Eliasian conceptualization of the civilizing process, while fundamental in his sociology, is too often seen as integral to figurational theory. Rather than categorizing Elias as a theorist of *the* civilizing process, it is more accurate to consider his earliest tome in the figurationalist library as a first step in thinking processually; *The Civilizing Process* (1978a) is but one case study in which Elias documents how physical bodies, emotions, groups, cultures and nation-states develop interdependently over time.

Third, at the heart of Elias's sociology is a belief in grounding any analysis of a contemporary phenomenon through an historical lens. The linchpin, to some degree, of Elias's viewpoint is that studying something that interests you necessarily involves grasping how it emerges over a long period of time. To be fair to Elias's sociological approach, people attracted to his theoretical sensitivities must develop what we might call a long-term sociological perspective.

Concluding thoughts

My perspective on sociology, the sociological enterprise and indeed social life, changed when I first read Elias's work. What impresses me in particular about him are the keen connections he makes between what you or I might see and experience as part of our daily lives and things that seem to be so distant from us. Elias's understanding of how people both produce their times and are products of their times is classic sociological insight. He is, of course, not the only sociologist to reach such a conclusion, but he did so in such a manner that explains how the very minutiae of social life are woven deeply into a long-term historical story. In the study of Parkour, for example, he helps me to understand how people simply do not pioneer, or come to, a practice accidentally. The contexts of our lives that we in part inherit and in part make draw us towards specific cultures. Our mindsets towards them are shaped by trends, patterns and forces stretching far back into our social histories – both as individual people and as societies. The kind of Parkour enthusiasm I studied with the crew in Hamilton only makes sociological sense in those historical, cultural, environmental and personal contexts.

Physical cultures like Parkour, and in this case a group who practise the original Natural Method, push us to de-individualize how we see adventurous practices and their relevance to people over long and short terms. For quite some time in the study of Western sport and physical activity we have recognized that athletic sojourns into the woods continue to be meaningful to people because they speak to and about the whole of the human experience. Elias and his figurational sociology help underline these theoretical connections.

Further reading

For anyone interested in reading more about the essential principles of figurational sociology, sociologists including Robert van Krieken, Stephen Mennell and Johan

Goudsblom have edited wonderful introductory books showcasing selections of Elias's primary writings. Among the most instructive and concise is:

Van Krieken, R. (1998) *Norbert Elias*, London: Routledge.

References

Atkinson, M. (2009) 'Parkour, anarcho-environmentalism and poiesis', *Journal of Sport and Social Issues*, 33(2), 169–94.

Atkinson, M. and Young, K. (2008) *Deviance and social control in sport*, Champaign, IL: Human Kinetics.

Dunning, E. (1999) *Sport matters*, London: Routledge.

Elias, N. (1978a) *The civilizing process*, Oxford: Basil Blackwell.

Elias, N. (1978b) *What is sociology?*, London: Hutchinson.

Elias, N. and Dunning, E. (1986) *The quest for excitement: Sport and leisure in the civilizing process*, Oxford: Basil Blackwell.

Goudsblom, J. (1977) *Sociology in the balance: A critical essay*, New York: Columbia University Press.

Maguire, J. (1993) 'Bodies, sport cultures and societies: A critical review of some theories in the sociology of the body', *International Review for the Sociology of Sport*, 28(1), 33–50.

Wheaton, B. (2012) *The cultural politics of lifestyle sports*, London: Routledge.

7

ERVING GOFFMAN

Sail training, interactionism and the 'total institution'

Ken McCulloch

This chapter explores the work of the Canadian-born sociologist Erving Goffman (1922–82). It draws on examples from the world of sail training to explore the ways sociological approaches such as interactionism and, in particular, Goffman's concept of the 'total institution' can help us to frame, interpret and analyse the situations in which adventure educators work. Goffman's work does not fit easily into any of the usual schemes for categorizing different sociological approaches, and he is often regarded as something of a maverick – someone who pursued his own ideas and preoccupations without much regard to what else may have been happening in the academic community around him. He is said to have been somewhat reclusive – the opposite of the celebrity academic – but is nevertheless regarded as one of the key figures in twentieth-century sociology.

Goffman's work covers a range of themes and contexts, but is always informed by a concern to understand the nature of human interaction. He might be understood as operating in the area of sociology that borders on social psychology. Although he is often described as a *symbolic interactionist*, he resisted labelling of that kind and only went as far as describing himself, in an interview near the end of his life, as an 'urban ethnographer' (Verhoeven, 1993). Goffman is best known for three sets of ideas. The first is the *interaction order* and its connection to what has become known as symbolic interactionism. Symbolic interactionism is a term used by many sociologists when referring to ways of studying social life that include Goffman's particular approach, and will be used throughout this chapter as I explore Goffman's contribution to the sociological understanding of outdoor adventure. The second, closely related, set of themes in Goffman's work are *dramaturgy* and 'performance' in everyday life. This chapter, however, concentrates mainly on his third important idea: the *total institution*.

Goffman's doctoral thesis was a study of life on a small island in the Shetland group, which lies north of the Scottish mainland. The focus of the study was on the ways people communicate and his analysis of conversational interaction as a 'social order'. This work formed the foundation for his book, published in 1956, *The Presentation of Self in Everyday Life*, in which he developed ideas about interaction, conversation and the ways in which people 'present' themselves through social 'performances' as a means of managing social relations. Although this exploration of what he called 'the interaction order' was the main focus of Goffman's work, he is well known for his work on psychiatric patients and stigma. The idea of the total institution was set out in *Asylums* (1961). This influential book was derived from a year-long period of fieldwork at a psychiatric hospital in Washington, DC. It explores the nature of 'total institutions', which, Goffman argues, might include mental hospitals, boarding schools, prisons and ships at sea.

The focus of this chapter is the use of Goffman's ideas as aids to understanding some aspects of social life. His symbolic interactionist approach is a useful way of thinking about, and analysing, social settings of any kind. For researchers thinking about outdoor and adventurous activities, Goffman's ideas about total institutions provide a powerful theoretical tool. Adventure activities often place participants in some degree of isolation from their normal life, as they take place in remote locations and because it is difficult for participants to separate themselves from the rest of their group. In the case of participation in a sail training voyage, this is one of the most important features; as soon as the vessel moves even a short distance from a harbour or quay, it becomes impossible, practically speaking, for an individual to leave the situation or for anyone to enter from outside.

The rest of this chapter offers an explanation of my own interest in and brief summaries of the key concepts of symbolic interactionism and of the total institution, before telling two 'sea stories' that explore ways in which the concept of the total institution can help us more deeply to understand the practice of sail training. Finally, the chapter introduces some more theoretical arguments about the use of these sociological concepts as tools for understanding social life.

Background

The examples in this chapter focus on what goes on aboard a sail training vessel. *Sail training* is a term that is used and understood differently according to context. It is sometimes used to indicate teaching of seamanship, but more often it refers to the practice of taking young people to sea in a sailing vessel with the intention that the participants will learn, grow and develop through that experience. I am employing the term in that second sense, although it is important to note that other terms are often used, such as youth sailing, youth work at sea or adventure sailing, to describe activities with similar aims and practices. Participants are generally teenagers or young adults.

The essential features of a sail training programme are:

• the use of sailing vessels of a size which can accommodate a group of young people and one or, usually, more members of staff living aboard for a period;

- time spent at sea – normally, but not exclusively, under sail power;
- motives which are concerned with participants' development as people.

The experience may have as one of its outcomes the learning of sailing and seamanship skills, but these are not generally considered to be primary aims. The conceptual boundary between sailing schools, which provide courses of technical instruction in sailing, and sail training organizations is not always clear-cut, but the key features identified above are sufficient as a definition for sail training.

Within the broad field of sail training, many important differences need to be recognized. These arise from varying ideas about the purpose of the work, and from a range of national and regional cultures and traditions. Programmes differ according to their specific aims. These differences include features such as the types of vessel used and the culture and practices that characterize particular approaches. In the UK, the smallest sail training vessels are yachts of around 10m in length and which carry perhaps two staff and four or five trainees; the largest are ships of 40m or even greater length, which may carry a dozen or more staff and thirty or forty trainees. The most common model of practice in the UK and most other countries uses vessels of around 20m that accommodate a dozen trainees and five or six staff.

Size is not the only kind of difference; the technologies by which sailing vessels operate range from very traditional to very modern, with many variants in between. The significance of the particular waters sailed, the length and duration of voyages and the weather conditions encountered all contribute to the variety of experiences available to participants.

I became involved in sail training in the early 1990s, having previously been professionally involved in working with young people for many years. A consistent thread of interest in outdoor activity formed an element of my professional practice; for example, in my first full-time youthwork post, I regularly took groups for camping weekends. I also worked on in-service training that helped colleagues to develop outdoor activity skills, as well as with climbing and mountaineering youth activity groups. From these origins, a strong interest in understanding the significance of educational work with young people in non-school settings had emerged. In a very real sense, my undertaking research in this area was the synthesis of these different strands of my own experiences as a youth worker, as an occasional outdoor educator, as a sail training practitioner and as a sociologist.

Symbolic interactionism and 'total institutions'

Sociology offers many different perspectives on human life. As we have seen in Chapter 1, these range from the macro-scale explanations of the influences on individual and community life at the level of nation states or economic systems (e.g. capitalism), to the micro-scale which focuses on aspects such as how people function in small groups. The area of sociology that this chapter explores is broadly concerned with understanding social interaction from the perspective of participants, and has affinities with social anthropology and social psychology.

So-called symbolic interactionist writers such as Goffman (1961) and William Foot Whyte (1981) provide examples of the kind of research which examines the ways people interact and make sense of their interactions in everyday situations. Researchers in this tradition seek to exploit the potential of sociological ethnography to explore meaning and to develop an account of social acts and settings. Sociological ethnography is a well-established research tradition and has drawn on a range of ideas and practices since its emergence within the Chicago School in the first half of the twentieth century (Deegan, 2001).

When studying a field of practice such as sail training, a key problem is to understand how naive young participants make sense of a new and profoundly unfamiliar setting, in terms of language, social behaviour and the physical environment. Researching such a setting involves collecting data about the meanings that participants attach to their experiences, in order to establish a grasp of the ways those individuals make sense of the situation. The research on which this chapter draws used a combination of interviews undertaken with participants during sail training voyages and observation of events and interactions aboard a number of sail training vessels (McCulloch, 2002). This was research undertaken, in Goffman's own phrase, as an 'observant participant' rather than as a participant observer (see Smith, 2006).

Goffman wrote *Asylums* (1961) following an extended period of ethnographic fieldwork in a mental hospital, where he observed and interacted with patients in order to try to understand their experiences in that situation. You might be forgiven for wondering why this might help with sociological enquiry into outdoor adventure! The reason this is important is that although Goffman's work focused, in this case, on the particular setting of the mental hospital, his findings led to a more widely useful set of ideas about social settings that share some characteristics with the research context. We call this principle *generalizability*, which means that the theory that emerges from research in one particular setting can help us to understand, or at least to think more carefully about, some other setting. So, for example, studying how leadership emerges and operates – or how conflict is dealt with – in a small group travelling through remote country might help us think about leadership in politics or in a workplace environment.

The main theoretical concept that we can draw from *Asylums* is the idea of the total institution. Goffman (1961) first defines the total institution as a 'place of residence and work where a large number of individuals, cut off from the wider society for an appreciable period of time, together lead an enclosed, formally administered round of life' (p. xiii). Goffman's analysis of the practices of mental hospitals in mid-twentieth-century America is interwoven with evidence regarding, for example, prisons, concentration camps, boarding schools, convents and crucially, in the present context, ships. In his analysis, a number of features of total institutions are proposed, including role differences within both staff and inmate groups, modes of recruitment of staff and inmates, permeability (e.g. the difference between social life and standards within and outside the boundary) and the destinations or 'social fate' of their 'graduates'. He describes the 'staff world' and the 'inmate world' in some detail and uses the concept of *institutional ceremony* to categorize particular kinds of events, which can be understood as staging 'a difference between two constructed categories of persons – a difference in social quality and moral character, a difference in perceptions of self and other' (Goffman, 1961, p. 104).

The following accounts provide powerful evidence of the significance of the institutional boundary inherent in sail training. The first concerns circumstances where the boundaries were compromised by action from outside the vessel, by the parents of young trainees. The second account is an example of a challenge to the boundary by a trainee from the inside. There is also a third type of breach in the institutional boundary, which can be conceptualized as withdrawal of authority. These two accounts can be understood as instances that bring the nature and characteristics of institutional boundaries into sharp focus.

These ethnographic 'sea stories' exemplify, respectively, the two main types of challenge to the boundary. Both events raised issues about the relationship of individuals to the collective, and the nature of trainees' commitment to or contract with the sail training context. The power of the evidence they represent resides unambiguously in their unusual nature and in the effects the events had on individuals and on the ship's company in each case.

'We thought we'd come and say hello'

The first type of challenge to the boundary seems to be less common, and was unintentional. The events described were unique in my experience and were judged very unusual by the highly experienced full-time skipper involved. This case explores the experiences of a voyage in *James Cook* from North Shields to Aberdeen. A combination of factors created the potential for a sequence of events which demonstrate quite dramatically how participants' perceptions of the voyage and their role in it can be altered when the boundaries are breached. In this case the challenge to the boundaries was created, albeit unintentionally, by action from outside the boat, by trainees' parents. It demonstrates, by comparing the experiences of two individual participants, how challenges to the institutional boundary from the outside can fundamentally change the nature of trainees' experiences.

James Cook is a seventy-foot ketch, and the trainees on board were a group of twelve- and thirteen-year-old teenagers from a school in the north-east of England. On the first day we made a fairly uneventful passage some twenty miles north from the Tyne. Quite a number of the trainees reported feeling seasick, several actually vomiting at various stages of the day. The following morning we headed further up the coast towards Eyemouth, not far from where the young trainees lived. In more comfortable sea conditions the teenagers began to participate quite energetically in learning to handle sails and to steer the boat under sail. We arrived in harbour at Eyemouth in the evening of the second day, at about 7.30pm. Dinner was being prepared, to be ready soon after tying up and securing the boat.

We arrived in Eyemouth to find that several sets of parents had decided to drive up and meet the boat 'just to say hello and see how you were all doing', as one put it. Our progress along the coast had been observed by some of the trainees' families, and from their perspective we had not disappeared over the horizon either literally or in the sense of moving beyond their immediate direct consciousness. Thinking about Goffman's description of what characterizes a total institution, we can see that the boundary usually created by the disappearance of the vessel from view had never been properly established, and the separation of the world inside the boat from the social world 'outside' had not been successfully created.

One of the trainees, R, had been mildly seasick the first day and still reported feeling nauseous some of the time on the second day. When he saw his mother, he told her that he wanted to get off the boat and was not at all keen to stay. The skipper talked with R and his mother for about fifteen or twenty minutes standing on the quay. R and his mother then went away and talked. R was evidently clear that he was not keen to go on, but the upshot of the discussion was that he decided or had been persuaded to stay on.

The incident presented a potential opportunity for this young person to go back to what was safe and known, the presence of his mother and of the family car making it clear to him that if he really wanted to, he could get off. The persuasion that was exercised was to encourage him to stay on, to 'give it a chance' and to stay with what he'd committed himself to. Staff subsequently learned that another trainee, P, had met his family and had had a similar conversation, but without anyone involving the boat's staff in any way, P eventually agreeing, with his father, to carry on 'for at least one more day'. For both these trainees the boundary between the social world of family and home and the institutional world of the ship had become blurred and ambiguous.

The following morning we made an offshore passage of fifty nautical miles to Montrose. Dinner and the washing up were finished at about 9pm. The trainees were told they could go ashore, that they should be back on the boat by 10.30pm and that they could also have a couple of hours ashore the following morning. At about 9.30pm several trainees who had been shopping for sweets returned; then at 10.30pm one of the trainees came to tell me 'P's dad is here to take him home'. It emerged that P had phoned his father not long after we had arrived to say that he wanted to go home.

During Friday he had given every impression of enjoying what he was doing, being interested and willing to participate in the life of the vessel. P's father turned up when the skipper and the other staff were away. The father said that he had promised the boy in Eyemouth that if he still wasn't happy being on the boat after another day, he would drive to wherever the boat was and take him home, and having made this promise to his son he felt he should keep his word. P confirmed that he wanted to go, took his belongings, which were already packed, got in the car with his father and off they went.

This illuminates the nature of institutional boundaries. The visible presence of mum or dad and the discussion about the possibility of getting off the boat and going home seemed to open the boundary that being a member of the ship's company normally creates. Once that possibility is opened up, they may choose to make use of it. We would not have expected this to happen if parents had not turned up in Eyemouth. This external challenge to the boundary is important because it is not simply a question of going into harbour and having the opportunity to go ashore. Rather, it is the realization that the boundary of the boat is a creation held together only by the consent of the participants. The presence of R's parents made it possible for him to see that boundary as one he could choose to ignore. By his own account he saw that possibility and considered it, and was persuaded not to cross. P, on the other hand, saw the permeability of the boundary and took that knowledge with him to the next port, acting on his awareness of the possibility by phoning his father and asking to be collected. (This incident occurred at a time just before mobile phones became widespread; sail training practitioners have adopted a variety of strategies in response to the spread of the new technology.)

The continued physical presence of the vessel in the awareness of interested outside observers can be understood as creating conditions where there was no effective strong boundary as seen from the outside. Their action then created the conditions for the revelation, for trainees, that the boundary around the vessel is (once in harbour) only maintained by the acquiescence of the participants.

The story of J

The second type of challenge to these boundaries is a fairly regular occurrence and involves the sustained expression, by one or more trainees, of a desire to get off the boat and go home. It is important to distinguish transient discontent, which is fairly common, from more sustained challenges. The former, usually appearing when people are seasick, tired and uncomfortable, is usually fairly brief, and not confined to trainees. The more sustained, and from the point of view of ships' staff, more problematic challenges are when one or more trainees demand to be put ashore, often withdrawing co-operation as a bargaining device. The second example presents a situation of this kind.

The focus of this instance is the way a single individual can create tensions and uncertainties for the whole ship's company through a challenge to the boundaries from the inside. J, a fifteen-year-old boy, was one of the trainees on a voyage aboard *Spirit of Fairbridge* on the west coast of Scotland. He decided after one full day aboard in challenging conditions that he wanted to get off the boat and go home to the south of England. His leaving would have extensive consequences. The long coach journey home for J meant that, due to his age, he would have to be accompanied by one of the two adult volunteers aboard. The other fifteen-year-old on the boat from the same area would also have to leave at the same time in order not to be travelling alone at the end of the voyage.

Not long after getting out of bed J began to express a desire to go home, saying he was not feeling well. He had been fairly seasick the previous night, as had most of the other trainees. After some discussion he agreed initially to stay on the boat for one more night. The rest of that day was spent at anchor, making some repairs and awaiting the favourable evening tide for the next leg of the voyage. By five in the evening, however, J had made his mind up that he was no longer willing to stay on the boat; he wanted to go home.

At that point it was clear that this challenge had potential major consequences for the voyage. The threat or desire to breach the boundaries by one person, might affect a number of other individuals. The situation was a fundamental preoccupation of everyone aboard individually for most of that day, and therefore for the company as a whole. Could we in fact proceed to our destination with only five or six trainees? Did the voyage plan need be revised with a different destination? These were all just speculations at that moment, illustrating very powerfully the difficulty created, and the significance of an individual choosing to or wishing to leave the boat. The management of the situation in this case was made easier by the position of the vessel at anchor. This maintained a physical boundary and prevented J from simply walking ashore, as he might have done had *Spirit* been moored alongside the pier. Eventually either J was persuaded to stay aboard or perhaps he came to realize himself that he was in a practical sense committed to staying with the boat for some time yet. The possibility of choice was, as Goffman describes, removed from him literally as well as symbolically on joining the institution that was the ship.

There is evidence here that the tension between concern for and with individuals can be in tension with concern for the whole, for the vessel and her company collectively. This tension between individual and collective interests is neither unique to the sail training environment nor only evident in a crisis such as J's. The parallel with other educational settings is evident, and the dilemma of individual versus collective welfare is familiar to most educators in schools and in less formal settings. This is often characterized as a problem of disproportionate attention: 'Teachers and others are aware of the time and effort which can be devoted to a small number of disaffected pupils, time which is, therefore, being denied the majority' (Munn et al., 2000, p. 43). In sail training this problem can be particularly acute, not so much in relation to attention being unevenly given to trainees but in relation to the tension between these concerns and the maritime imperatives. Trainees can require particular attention from staff for all kinds of reasons, and the management of this tension is as familiar to sail training staff as it is to any primary school teacher.

More generally it appears that the nature and extent of trainees' preparation for the experience are significant in relation to potential challenges. Folk wisdom among practitioners suggests this, and observations both during the specific fieldwork and more broadly tend to support this view. Challenges to the institutional boundary in this common form of a demand to terminate the experience associated with the withdrawal of co-operation seem nearly always to come from younger trainees – particularly young teenage boys – who have had limited opportunities to develop an advance understanding of what they might be letting themselves in for. Such cases also often appear to involve trainees who have acquiesced to participation at adult suggestion, rather than having authentically given reasonably well-informed consent.

Conclusion: institutionality, communality, power and ideology

The evidence that cases such as these provide clearly supports the view that participation in sail training is indeed both a powerful experience and a significant event for participants (McCulloch *et al.*, 2010). The argument being made in this chapter is that the inescapable mutuality of seafaring is the central feature of the sail training experience. Boundaries are created and maintained physically, temporally and through the emergence of authentic dependence on one's shipmates. The bounded nature of the social setting provided by a ship at sea can be interpreted in two main ways. It can be seen as a *community* in the 'warmly persuasive' sense (Williams, 1976) or, alternatively, as an *institution* in the colder and more austere sense that the term usually implies. To understand these categories as dichotomous may, however, be unhelpful. To see community and institution as points on a continuum is also tempting, although it does ignore some important problems. It is more useful to think of 'community' and 'institution' as ideal types, as theoretical, heuristic constructs that provide analytical lenses through which to examine specific contexts.

Community is understood increasingly as an intermediate social space where individual agency and social structure come into dialectical contact (Martin, 2000) and where change is possible. Institutions may have some of the features of communities and may readily be understood as sites for individuals and social structure to come into contact. What institutionality means, however, is that change, both in respect of individuals and for social relations, is much more constrained. The institution constrains choice, not just for the inmate, patient or trainee but equally for the staff who exercise authority in the name of the institution.

In considering the usefulness of these ideas for the analysis of sail training, or of seafaring more generally, Gerstenberger's (1996) critique of Goffman is important. The argument advanced was essentially that historical evidence regarding the practices of shipboard life in the German merchant marine over three centuries undermines the claim that there are strong parallels between shipboard life and that of asylums, prisons or barracks. Gerstenberger argues that it is the use of particular economic and managerial strategies that 'determines the extent of authority and hierarchy aboard merchantmen' (p. 175). The fundamental flaw in Gerstenberger's case is the very narrow reading placed on Goffman. The historical evidence offered is intriguing and valuable for the insights it offers into the growth of hierarchy and the institutionalization of authority. Nevertheless, the isolation imposed by a ship at sea, from a sociological viewpoint, makes it far more similar to than different from a monastery or a military unit, and thus a *total institution*.

Life aboard a sail training vessel is uniquely inescapable; an individual can only isolate themselves in a very limited and temporary manner. In that respect, a residential centre or an uninhabited landscape that one is travelling through always offers a more permeable boundary. An individual can hurry ahead, lag behind or simply walk away from camp to find some temporary detachment from the group. The concept of the total institution provides a framework for thinking about relationships, practices and issues arising in such a context. More broadly, Goffman's work and that of other interactionist sociologists provides a powerful tool for the analysis of the social milieu in which outdoor education takes place.

Further reading

For an account of Goffman's life and sociological work, see Greg Smith's *Erving Goffman* (referenced below).

If you are interested in exploring the idea of the 'total institution' a bit further, you should read Goffman's *Asylums* and Foucault's *Discipline and Punish* (referenced below). The latter is quite a difficult read but is worth the effort. The title is also notable, in this context, for having been used (in the original French *Surveiller et punir*) as the name for a difficult climb in the Gorges du Verdon.

To find out more about sail training you might start with my article 'More than mere adventure: Sail training as education' (McCulloch *et al.*, 2010) (referenced below).

References

Deegan, M.J. (2001) 'The Chicago School of ethnography', in P. Atkinson, A. Coffey, S. Delamont, J. Lofland and L. Lofland (eds), *Handbook of ethnography* (pp. 11–25), London, Sage.

Foucault, M. (1991) *Discipline and punish: The birth of the prison*, London: Penguin.

Gerstenberger, H. (1996) 'Men apart: The concept of "total institution" and the analysis of seafaring', *International Journal of Maritime History*, 8, 173–82.

Goffman, E. (1956) *The presentation of self in everyday life*, Garden City, NY: Doubleday.

Goffman, E. (1961) *Asylums: Essays on the social situation of mental patients and other inmates*, Garden City, NY: Doubleday.

McCulloch, K. (2002) 'Four days before the mast: A study of sail training in the UK', unpublished PhD thesis, University of Edinburgh.

McCulloch, K., McLaughlin, P., Allison, P., Edwards, V. and Tett, L. (2010) 'More than mere adventure: Sail training as education', *Oxford Review of Education*, 36(6), 661–76.

Munn, P., Lloyd, G. and Cullen, M.A. (2000) *Alternatives to exclusion from school*, London: Paul Chapman.

Smith, G. (2006) *Erving Goffman*, London: Routledge.

Verhoeven, J.C. (1993) 'An interview with Erving Goffman, 1983', *Research on Language and Social Interaction*, 26(3), 317–48.

Whyte, W.F. (1981) *Street corner society*, Chicago, IL: University of Chicago Press.

Williams, R. (1976) *Keywords: A vocabulary of culture and society*, London: Collins.

8

PIERRE BOURDIEU

Habitus, field and capital in rock climbing

Simon Beames and John Telford

This chapter focuses on the work of the French sociologist Pierre Bourdieu. During his career, Bourdieu wrote prolifically on a remarkably wide range of issues in society. As examining all of his work in one chapter is not possible, we will focus on three of Bourdieu's concepts that will enable us to see the social world through his eyes: habitus, field and capital. We will use examples from the world of rock climbing to illustrate the theory.

Biography

Pierre Bourdieu was born into unremarkable and relatively humble circumstances in the south-west of France in 1930. At the time of his death in 2002, however, he was firmly established as one of the most influential thinkers of his generation, and also as one of the most outspoken and energetic intellectual activists of the last twenty years. He enjoyed a stellar academic career and taught at a number of elite institutions. In 1981 he became a professor at the most prestigious institution in the French university system: the Collège de France. In 1995 he was awarded a gold medal by the National Centre for Scientific Research. One of his many books, *Distinction: A social critique of the judgement of taste*, was named by the International Sociological Association as one of the ten most important sociological works of the twentieth century. Remarkably, it was not until the 1980s that Bourdieu's work became commonly known in the English-speaking world. By the late 1980s he had become one of the most frequently cited French social scientists in the United States.

Bourdieu did not confine himself to an academic career spanning philosophy, sociology and ethnology. His insistence on the importance of connecting theory with real life is evidenced by his contribution to discussions and activism in a wide range of areas, including art, literature, education, language, culture, television, sport, anti-globalization and the rights of workers. The main thread that ran through his work was an interest in the ways that culture and class combine to create power.

Bourdieu's theory of social practice

One reason that we are drawn to Bourdieu's work is that we find some of his key concepts very helpful for understanding everyday social behaviour in general, and outdoor adventure specifically. As explained in Chapter 1, two broad schools of thought have traditionally existed in sociology. Each attempts to provide a framework for understanding the way people think and act in the social world. On the one hand, there are those who see human behaviour as being heavily influenced by external forces. On the other hand, there are those who believe that individuals have a high degree of 'agency', as they are largely in control of the decisions they make. The former is often referred to as a structuralist or objectivist point of view. That is to say, there are objective social structures that influence the way people behave. The latter is often referred to as a subjectivist stance, as every individual is consciously and subjectively capable of directing their own thoughts and actions without being overly influenced by external social forces (see, for example, May and Powell, 2008).

Let's imagine a climber decided to chisel some new holds on El Capitan's iconic route 'The Nose'. This would undoubtedly cause an uproar that would reverberate across the international climbing community. But why? There are no laws against chipping. Relatively few people will ever climb the route and those that do climb it aren't obliged to use the chipped holds if they don't want to. It is even arguable that after a couple of years of weathering the chipped holds will no longer be visually obtrusive. If large-scale quarrying is common place in the world's industrial mines, then what's the big fuss over a little chipping on a rock climb? Well, it is clearly not a question of how many people will come into contact with the chipped holds, and nor is it a question of comparative physical impact on the natural world. It is entirely a question of the values and assumptions that a dominant culture ascribes to the relationship between climbers and iconic routes.

A structuralist perspective on this scenario would suggest that as new people enter the climbing community, they are gradually socialized into adopting the accepted, and often unquestioned, practices and beliefs. These normalized behaviours are subtly communicated through club meets, magazine articles, photographs, books, blogs and every other way that climbers interact. The climber responsible for the chipping must have come from a different community with very different traditions from those he or she encounters in Yosemite. A subjectivist perspective, on the other hand, would contend that every individual climber has come to an ethical position on the question of chipping holds through a free and rational process of consideration.

Bourdieu, however, suggests that neither a structuralist nor a subjectivist viewpoint adequately accounts for the complex workings of the social world. It is not the inevitable fate of human beings to adopt the values and behaviours of their social environment; nor are human beings entirely capable of perceiving the social influences on them and making independent, rational decisions on that basis. Bourdieu asserts that the opposition between structuralism and subjectivism is a false dichotomy that impedes our understanding of the social world. He notes that: 'Of all the oppositions that artificially divide social science, the most fundamental, and the most ruinous, is the one that is set up between subjectivism and objectivism' (Bourdieu, 1990, p. 25).

So, if objectivism and subjectivism won't do, what is the alternative? This is where Bourdieu's work starts to fascinate us. He proposes that human agency and objective social structures exist in a dynamic, interdependent relationship (Bourdieu, 1977, 1990). Understood in this way, people are able to think, choose and act, thanks to their human capacity to be aware of themselves in relation to other people and institutions of the social world (such as education systems, established religions or sporting organizations). However, this ability for self-determination exists within certain limits that are established by the common practices and structures of the social world.

In the UK, the predominant attitude amongst climbers is that bolting should only take place according to very specific guidelines. This is in order to maintain a tradition that values a 'leave no trace' approach to the rock, upholds the value of adventurous climbing whereby the leader places protection, and honours the possibility that what cannot be climbed by this traditional method today may well be possible in the future (see Lewis, 2000). If a UK climber schooled in this tradition were to move to France, he or she would experience a much more liberal approach to the use of bolts, which is supported by an equally logical rationale. It is likely that this new 'normal' behaviour would highlight for the individual the way that their previous opinions, thoughts and practices had been influenced by the dominant values of the UK climbing community. For example, bolting a run-out pitch on a classic mountain route would be unthinkable in the UK, whereas in France it would be perfectly reasonable. However, it is only unthinkable in the UK because a particular set of social values encourages the belief that it is unthinkable. Because it is unthinkable, bolting is 'unavailable' even as a potential course of action. Therefore, it is possible for an individual to self-impose limits on his or her behaviour at the same time as believing that his or her freedom to act has not been restricted. This example illustrates the complex interplay between the influence of social structures and the subjective ability of individuals to direct their lives.

Let's take another example. Imagine that Harriet and Vanessa (both seventeen years old) join an indoor climbing wall in their home town. With no previous experience of climbing or the climbing world, Harriet and Vanessa will come into contact for the first time with the established patterns of behaviour of the club members. Harriet and Vanessa will encounter new ways of speaking, behaving and dressing that are commonly expressed within their new community of friends. In addition, they will also be exposed to the predominant attitudes or values that are foundational to the culture of the club. For example, they will encounter dominant views on whether to use a Grigri or an ATC for belaying, attitudes towards safety and risk, beliefs about what is cool and not cool, and pick up cues regarding which members of the club carry high status and the reasons for this. As Harriet and Vanessa have had no previous experience of climbing culture, it is difficult for them to critique the behaviour and values of the climbing culture around them. If the culture of the club suggests to them in various ways, both explicit and implicit, that completing a climb without falling or resting on the rope is the 'purest' form of success, it is likely that they will accept and adopt this value.

To summarize, the basic notion to which Bourdieu calls our attention is that human behaviour is directly related to culture, social structures and power. To help us further understand this relationship and how it relates to outdoor adventure, we need to consider three of Bourdieu's important concepts: *habitus*, *field* and *capital*.

Habitus

Bourdieu (1990, p. 65) once asked: 'how can behaviour be regulated without being the product of obedience to rules?' This question was motivated by a belief that all cultures reveal patterns of conforming behaviour that cannot be explained in terms of explicitly stated laws, such as those relating to road speed limits, violent behaviour or paying income tax. These patterns are driven by objective social structures that are not explicitly stated or justified. How do cultural practices develop to the point of being unquestioned, and, perhaps more importantly, unquestionable, social norms?

Bourdieu suggests that through the experiences of everyday life (particularly formative experiences in the early years) individuals unconsciously adopt the social patterns and norms that surround them. Notions of what is 'right' and appropriate become ingrained, instinctive patterns of thought and behaviour. Bourdieu refers to these instinctive tendencies towards certain behaviours as *habitus*.

Habitus can be described as 'the values and dispositions gained from our cultural history that generally stay with us across contexts' (Webb *et al.*, 2002, p. 36). In other words, whether I am watching the Royal Ballet, working in a factory, dining out with my very wealthy cousins, sitting in a lecture at university or volunteering at a homeless shelter, my instinctive notions and actions with regard to what is normal, appropriate, interesting, funny, outrageous or distasteful will remain more or less the same. In addition, habitus is both individual and collective. Every individual person develops their own instinctive dispositions but, at the same time, groups of people from the same or a similar social environment will share a similar group habitus, and will share what Bourdieu terms *doxa*: foundational, unconsidered cultural beliefs.

Doxa encourages not only the acceptance of the way things are but, moreover, gives us a sense that the way things are is the way they ought to be (Jenkins, 2002, p. 156). This answers the question from two paragraphs earlier about how cultural practices develop; over time, values, attitudes and behaviours become ingrained into individuals' patterns of thought and action. Habitus is thus exhibited in every aspect of an individual's life. Interpersonal relationships, life expectations and choices, politics, religion, speech, gait, ways of dressing, the names we give our children – to name but a handful – all stem from and reflect the habitus.

We can see that the habitus is both a social context that influences what people think and do, and a way of explaining their particular dispositions. One way of thinking about dispositions for Bourdieu (1989) is that certain values and beliefs become thought of as 'common sense' (p. 19). However, if you have ever spent any time thinking about the concept of common sense, you will no doubt have come to the conclusion that it is easily undermined by the simple question: common to whom? So, while having bolted belay stations on a trad route in Red Rocks may be common sense to folk in the south-west of the United States, having no bolts whatsoever would be common sense to those in North Wales. Common sense and 'instinctive knowledge' come from the values that we have absorbed through living in our specific social contexts and will always have the potential to be entirely 'uncommon' in many other social contexts.

Let us return to our two climbers, Harriet and Vanessa, and assume that they share a very similar cultural and socio-economic background. As very close friends, they have also shared many experiences. Thus, their exposure to the various habituses of their upbringing, related to the cultures of their family, their school, their soccer team and their church, result in the individual habitus of each young woman being very similar. Now, imagine that when they finish secondary school, they decide to spend six months climbing at Smith Rock in Oregon. Here they encounter the habitus of the climbing community, which has similarities to and differences from the habitus of their climbing wall club. Living in a tent village with other climbers for months at a time involves exposure to all of the unwritten and unspoken social structures of that community over an extended, and probably very intense, period of time. Quite often, these structures manifest themselves as social 'norms' of what is valued and what behaviours are implicitly expected. Examples of what is valued might be a strict code for 'onsighting' a climb, left-wing politics, reggae music, and a welcoming attitude towards newly arrived, aspiring climbers. The local climbing habitus, then, will naturally confront Harriet and Vanessa's own attitudes and behaviours concerning climbing ethics, politics, music and how to treat young newcomers.

One aspect of the habitus that is interesting to consider is its transferability and durability. If, as Bourdieu argues, individuals are exposed to a range of different habituses over their lifetime, one might expect that all of the different values and dispositions will mingle together with the result that the habitus of one person shares little in common with that of anyone else. This would result in a constantly shifting amalgamation of instincts and behaviours that would make it difficult to identify any durable or ingrained social patterns in individuals or in groups of people. So, when Harriet and Vanessa move to the hippy-ish collective of Smith Rock for the summer, to what extent will they carry with them the individualist, career-motivated and elitist ways that were built up over years of growing up in a very affluent, middle-class section of society in Connecticut? Equally, to what extent will their attitudes and behaviours be influenced by the new social environment of the climbing community, with its vast collection of explicit and implicit norms?

Bourdieu (1977) argues that we are influenced most by the formative experiences of early life. This is not surprising as, particularly in early childhood, we are least questioning of the environment and practices that surround us. In addition, it is very common for people to spend their childhood years in the same geographical location, same familial structure and same social surroundings. Thus, when we are least aware of unconscious social influences and most exposed to a stable, relatively unchanging environment, we are most likely to develop the durable, instinctive dispositions that Bourdieu suggests form the habitus.

So far, we have argued that the habitus formed in our early years is highly influential in shaping our thoughts and actions for the rest of our life. If we were to return to our earlier discussion regarding structuralism and subjectivism, this would seem to suggest that Bourdieu falls firmly in the camp of the structuralists. However, we know that Bourdieu believes that human beings have a degree of conscious control (agency) over their lives, and the ability to step beyond the 'norm' and challenge or reject the dominant doxa (cultural beliefs).

Harriet and Vanessa have been exposed to the habitus of the climbing community in two different ways. The first consisted of one year as members of a climbing club near their homes. Let us say that this involved three hours once a week at the climbing gym. The second consisted of six months of living in a community away from their home town and with all the influences and expectations that entails. Would we expect the habitus of Harriet and Vanessa to be at all affected in the first scenario, given that habitus is durable across different social contexts? Is it possible that the habitus of Harriet and Vanessa is sufficiently durable to remain intact when they move to Oregon? In each scenario the new set of social circumstances that Harriet and Vanessa encounter can be described in Bourdieu's terms as a new *field* – the second of his concepts that we are examining in this chapter. Moving into different fields, each with its own identifiable habitus, creates the opportunity for new values and dispositions to be incorporated into the individual's habitus (Webb *et al.*, 2002, p. 37) at both a conscious and an unconscious level. We will now explore the concept of field in greater depth.

Field

Bourdieu (1989) uses the term *field* (or *cultural field*) to describe structured, social contexts that comprise rules and practices that engender particular ways of being and thinking. Climbing, education, music, religion, art and politics are examples of fields. Each field has its own specific logic, traditions of necessary behaviour, and networks of relations that are created and maintained by both individuals and institutions. It is within these cultural fields that the habitus develops as a product of what is accepted as logical, appropriate and relevant within that field. It is these objective structures that will influence the way Harriet and Vanessa think during their time trying to climb hard routes at Smith Rock. As we can see, there is much more to their trip than having fun and becoming better climbers – although they may not be entirely aware of this!

For example, it may be that Harriet and Vanessa's school and home background was one where high test scores were considered very important. Those who gained high test scores were praised, accorded status in the community, and received material reward. Whether or not Harriet and Vanessa were students who achieved high test scores, Bourdieu's theory suggests that they will be affected by this cultural value and it will be absorbed into their habitus. In the new cultural field of climbing, this 'test score' aspect of their habitus may manifest itself in a situation whereby even if the climbing community places no value on how hard somebody can climb, Harriet and Vanessa will instinctively be drawn into feelings and behaviours associated with what grade they are, or are not, able to climb. Their instinctive disposition will be to unconsciously revert to the values of their habitus when they consider their own or others' ability on the rock, even if, consciously, they no longer wish to espouse these values.

Harriet and Vanessa's habitus, at a less-than-conscious level, resists the cultural values embedded in the habitus of the climbing community. However, at the same less-than-conscious level it is also slowly modified. So, it might be that little by little the more outdoor lifestyle of the tent village climbing community becomes not just manageable, or even comfortable, but instinctively preferable to the more indoor way of life of their upbringing. Bourdieu (1977, pp. 78–9) argues that this process happens in such a subtle yet powerful way that human beings are capable of subconsciously reconfiguring their past to fit with their present.

These examples of one habitus confronting another refer to interactions at an unconscious level. However, habitus can also be impacted at a conscious level. Although socio-cultural structures can be very powerful, they are also human creations and, as such, they are vulnerable to examination and challenge. Human beings do possess the capacity to take a step back, view a situation with fresh eyes, and determine to do things differently. The key to a new perspective on life becoming embedded in the habitus lies in the *doing*, or what Bourdieu (1977) refers to as the 'practice', of everyday social life. Simply having the new vision or understanding at an intellectual level is not sufficient to impact upon an individual's instinctive dispositions; it needs to be lived out and experienced over and over again. The opportunity for this, of course, is made more or less possible by the dominant surrounding culture.

New cultural fields also highlight certain attitudes or actions of the habitus that are not 'useful'. If the dominant attitude within the climbing community is that all institutions of authority are not to be trusted and anyone who thinks otherwise is foolishly naive, it is likely that Harriet and Vanessa will become more amenable to the dominant point of view. This is because people have the capacity to understand 'the rules of the game' (Bourdieu, 1977), or the conventions of the social situations they inhabit, and modify their dispositions and values accordingly as a means of improving their position within a field.

To return to our earlier question of the relative influence of each of the two climbing community scenarios – indoor club and tent village – we can see that the latter is likely to have the greater effect on the two new climbers. The scenario involving eating, playing and sleeping at Smith Rock provides greater opportunities for the habitus to be influenced at both conscious and unconscious levels due to the intense nature of the experience, and the removal of a competing cultural field. This may seem obvious or 'common sense', but Bourdieu's explanation helps us to understand at a theoretical level how an extended period of time in a new and different community is more likely to significantly influence an individual than short-term, regular exposure.

Up to this point we have stated that fields are structured social contexts that are made up of particular values, institutions, and ways of being. We have also stated that habitus develops as a result of the qualities of a field. However, we have not yet discussed how the logic, the networks of relations, and traditional behaviours of a field come into being or are maintained. This brings us to the third and final of Bourdieu's concepts we wish to discuss: capital.

Capital

An essential feature of a field is what Bourdieu (1986) refers to as the forms of capital within it. Capital is anything that is designated as being of value within a given field. Bourdieu identifies four kinds of capital: economic capital (money, property), cultural capital (knowledge, skills, aesthetic preferences), social capital (informal interpersonal networks) and symbolic capital (prestige, recognition) (Bourdieu, 1986, 1989).

An interesting aspect of capital is the way in which it is context specific. What is regarded as capital in one set of social circumstances may not be in another. Bourdieu (1993) reminds us that 'capital is effective in relation to a particular field' (p. 73). Someone who regularly solos 5.12 may possess significant capital and, therefore perhaps, a high degree of power, respect and choice in the field of rock climbing. However, this symbolic capital of being a bold rock climber is probably not transferable to the cultural fields of sculpture, French cuisine or archaeology. The people within these fields might not fully understand what free soloing was, and might not care. On the other hand, it can be possible to transfer capital from one field to another. Arnold Schwarzenegger is perhaps a master of this game, as he first 'traded' his body-building success for a career in Hollywood, and then used these forms of capital to enter the world of politics. In any given field the amount of power a person or group enjoys depends upon the capital they possess. In turn, the greater the amount of capital possessed, the more able a person or group is to influence what is considered to be of value.

Bourdieu argues that individuals and groups struggle within fields to improve their standing in relation to the capital that defines the field (Bourdieu, 1989, 1993). The cultural norms and rules of a field are a consequence of the social conflicts that occur within it. These conflicts centre first around what constitutes legitimate capital (what is desirable or of value) and, second, how that capital can be accessed and employed to people's advantage. What is perhaps most fascinating about this situation is how the rules of the game can be dominated – and even manipulated – by those with power. Power comes from possessing capital!

It is important to keep in mind, therefore, that fields are not rigid, fixed social environments. The outcome of the constant struggle for capital among the members of the field is that the dominant, commonly accepted perception of what is considered as valuable, desirable and normal is constantly shifting. Usually this is a gradual and subtle evolution, but occasionally it can be dramatic and sudden. Webb *et al.* (2002) state that 'fields are fluid and dynamic, mainly because they are always being changed both by internal practices and politics' (p. 28). As a direct result, what constitutes capital and how this capital is used are also ever-changing. While today the rules of the game in one climbing area might deem it acceptable to use a 'stick clip' to clip the first bolt on a route, they might not in a year from now if people possessing sufficient capital are able to alter the dominant value in this field of struggle.

Now let us return to Bourdieu's concept of the habitus. Consider the above idea of 'fluidity' in combination with the ways by which the habitus can change and evolve. It is possible to see how a field is both the cause and the effect of habitus, which is, in turn, both created by, and creator of, fields. Habitus and field exist in symbiotic relation with each other. A field is produced and maintained by the individuals and institutions within it, and the habitus results from the absorption of the structures of the field into the individuals' ways of being – in thought and action. It is through this relationship between field and habitus that Bourdieu proposes to have transcended the dualism of subjectivist and objectivist approaches to social practice. The behaviour of human beings in the social world – social practice – is thus understood as a dynamic, interdependent relationship between individual agency and the rules and practices of cultural fields.

Conclusions

Even if you understand the 'Bourdieu basics' as described in this chapter, how does this help our understanding of the world of outdoor adventure – or even just *the world*? Well, we suggest that Bourdieu's three concepts give us a language that enables us to have a deeper and more meaningful discussion about the world in which we live. Armed with this language we are more able to have a sophisticated debate about how we are able to influence, and be influenced by, the social circumstances that characterize life at the crag, in the living room or in the lecture hall.

We know that Bourdieu argues that all humans are heavily influenced by the habitus. The habitus is shaped by our socio-cultural experiences and accounts for our 'common-sense' thinking. We also know that people possess different forms of capital (e.g. symbolic, cultural, economic) and that what is considered to be capital varies from field to field. Appropriate forms of capital can be used to access resources and power within a given field (or site of cultural struggle). Finally, we know that what serves as capital is not fixed; what is deemed valuable by people is constantly being defined and re-defined. Human beings are constrained by the social rules of fields which they inhabit. However, to varying degrees, we all exert self-serving influence over the 'rules of the game' that characterize our cultural fields, irrespective of whether we abide by these rules, bend them or try to change them.

We encourage you to re-examine your various social worlds through Bourdieu's three concepts outlined in this chapter. Although the concepts of habitus, field and capital are understandable and useful in and of themselves, we argue that, when used together, they become a particularly useful set of tools for analysing the various social situations in which we find ourselves. The next time you go climbing, take a look around and see if you can use these three concepts to better understand what people are doing and why.

Further reading

Of the references listed below, read Webb *et al.* (2002) for a very accessible overview of Bourdieu's work. May and Powell (2008) will help to contextualize Bourdieu within the broader field of social theory. Try Bourdieu's paper on 'Social space and symbolic power' (1989) as your first read of something by the man himself.

Finally, the following articles provide further examples of Bourdieu's concepts being used to increase understanding of the worlds of outdoor adventure and of sport.

Bourdieu, P. (1978) 'Sport and social class', *Social Science Information*, 17(6), 819–40.
Fletcher, R. (2008) 'Living on the edge: The appeal of risk sports for the professional middle class', *Sociology of Sport Journal*, 25(3), 310–30.
Kay, J. and Laberge, S. (2002) 'Mapping the field of "AR": Adventure racing and Bourdieu's concept of field', *Sociology of Sport Journal*, 19(1), 25–46.
Kay, J. and Laberge, S. (2002) 'The "new" corporate habitus in adventure racing', *International Review for the Sociology of Sport*, 37(1), 17–36.
Swanson, L. (2009) 'Soccer fields of cultural [re]production: Creating "good boys" in suburban America', *Sociology of Sport Journal*, 26(3), 404–24.

References

Bourdieu, P. (1977) *Outline of a theory of practice*, Cambridge: Cambridge University Press.
Bourdieu, P. (1986) 'The forms of capital', in J. Richardson (ed.), *Handbook of theory of research for the sociology of education* (pp. 241–58), Westport, CT: Greenwood Press.
Bourdieu, P. (1989) 'Social space and symbolic power', *Sociological Theory*, 7(1), 14–25.
Bourdieu, P. (1990) *The logic of practice*, trans. R. Nice, Stanford, CA: Stanford University Press.
Bourdieu, P. (1993) *Sociology in question*, London: Sage.
Jenkins, R. (2002) *Pierre Bourdieu*, London: Routledge.

Lewis, N. (2000) 'The climbing body, nature and the experience of modernity', *Body and Society*, 6(3–4), 58–80.

May, T. and Powell, J.L. (2008) *Situating social theory*, Maidenhead: Open University Press.

Webb, J., Schirato, T. and Danaher, G. (2002) *Understanding Bourdieu*, London: Sage.

9

ANTHONY GIDDENS

Structuration theory and mountaineering

Paul Beedie

This chapter explores ways in which the work of the British sociologist Anthony Giddens can be used as a theoretical lens to more clearly understand the complex social world of mountaineering. Giddens has been a prolific writer over the last forty years, with hundreds of papers and chapters, as well as over thirty books, to his name. Clearly, such productivity cannot be considered in detail here, so the intention is to develop connections with the work he produced in the middle part of his career – notably *structuration theory* and its developments into the key concepts of reflexivity, self identity and lifestyle. In some ways, Giddens' central concern with the reconciliation of social structures and individual agency recalls the work of Pierre Bourdieu (see Chapter 8); however, the scope of Giddens' theorizing, in particular his concerns with risk society and processes of globalization as well as his emphasis upon resources and how they shape power relations, suggest a broader potential application to social theory.

Biography

Anthony Giddens was born in Edmonton, north London, in 1938. He worked under Dunning and Elias at the University of Leicester and was thus influenced by their figurational sociology (see Chapter 6), before he advanced his interest in the sociology of class and power that was to culminate in the publication of *The Constitution of Society* in 1984. It was his time at Cambridge University, and the founding of Polity Press, that facilitated his key texts *The Consequences of Modernity* (1990) and *Modernity and Self Identity* (1991). His move back to London as director of the London School of Economics in 1997 raised his profile as a public intellectual and led to a close relationship with Tony Blair. Giddens' interest in 'lifestyle politics' is rooted in his proposal of an alternative to a state-dominated Left and a market-dominated Right. In *Modernity and Self Identity* (1991), he suggests that people take a more active role in self-government by what he calls a 'democratising of democracy' (Stevenson, 2012, p. 49). It is his most developed work to date concerning the dynamic relationship between social institutions (structure) and individuals (agency) in defining the modern social world.

Giddens has been described as the 'last great modernist' because of his disinclination to accept the cultural relativism of post-modernity. Instead, he considers the complex world today as experiencing 'high' or 'radical' modernity – an intensification of life brought about by developments in transport, technology and industrialization. As the social world is attuned to these (and other) defining parameters, mountaineering, which originated as an organized sport in the nineteenth century, can be viewed as a product of these social conditions. This chapter will focus on Giddens' structuration theory (1984), in which he sets out to reconcile the relationship between structure and agency in the continuous process of interaction and knowledge generation. Giddens has not written specifically about sport and leisure, although his original MA thesis was about football. Nevertheless, his work has considerable potential to inform investigations of sport, leisure and adventure participation. The discussion in this chapter is particularly concerned with adventure and will be illustrated with examples from climbing and mountaineering.

Giddens, the modern world and adventure

Giddens (1990) suggests that the modern world broadly coincides with the period from the mid-eighteenth century to the present, and is characterized by significant ongoing changes in the organization of society – some of which are accelerating in radical ways. One consequence of modernity has been rapid industrialization and its commensurate processes of urbanization and commercialization. With a growing concentration of people in towns and cities in the nineteenth century, class began to structure British society and remains evident today. In particular, as Weber illustrated (see Chapter 4), an emergent middle class became increasingly influential in the control of education and the distribution of resources more generally.

Part of the middle class's energy was directed towards a counter-industrial movement that drew directly from the 'back to nature' philosophy of Jean-Jacques Rousseau. In this respect, the antithesis of scientific and engineering advances was articulated through an artistic interest in the attractions of wild places, which was epitomized as Romanticism and captured by Wordsworth's seminal publication *Guide to the English Lakes* in 1810. Wordsworth found the pace of life and the authenticity of living close to nature in the English Lake District to be a suitable alternative lifestyle in a modern world that was constantly 'in motion' and increasingly pragmatic, rational, production-orientated and ultimately alienating; being outdoors in wild places appeared to offer a grounded reality and thus a chance to locate one's 'authentic self'. Such a vision proved attractive to the middle classes, who articulated the sentiments of Romanticism in books and other art forms, and it continues to inform and shape their engagement with all adventure activities. It was also attractive to the working classes, who took to exploring hills and moors as an escape from the drudgery of factory production, because it offered a sense of stability – a kind of social anchor – in a modern world that Giddens (1990, p. 53) describes as 'like being aboard a careering juggernaut . . . rather than being in a carefully controlled and well driven car'.

There are three themes in what follows, namely, identity, lifestyle and risk. These are implicit in the overarching ambition of using structuration theory to understand the relationship between people and the social structures that organize our lives. For Giddens (1991), it is the power that comes from the differences between people, and between social organizations, that determines how we fit in the social world. The notion of identity and lifestyle become choices we can make; pictures, maps, guidebooks and specialist climbing and backpacking equipment are freely available in the developed world. Furthermore, we are constantly monitoring our place in the world; for example, we can wear down duvet jackets and hiking shoes as fashion statements even when we are nowhere near the mountains. Additionally, we can 'play' with risk because all mountaineering involves risk in the 'doing' of the sport and in the extent to which we identify in a social sense with the sport. Wordsworth was a poet who captured the ideas of escape to wild nature in his artistically creative work. Giddens is a social theorist whose work can help us understand how the modern world functions socially and politically, and these three themes of identity, lifestyle and risk, and the idea of power connected to resources to control one's life, are each useful in doing so.

The reasons why Giddens' work on the theory of *structuration* (1984) and the *Consequences of Modernity* (1990) continues to be relevant to understanding adventure today are as follows. First, adventure constitutes a significant social institution which has 'traditions' that are being challenged by the rapid and unprecedented changes of the late modern world. Second, adventure is a socially constructed enactment of activity that brings together relations of power that define social and spatial boundaries. Third, one 'consequence' of modernity is the separation of time and space, which, in the context of adventure, means that distant places such as the Himalayas might become more familiar than our local hills. This separation from historical roots has significant consequences for our sense of identity. And fourth, adventure is connected to 'risk' and risk (of all kinds, including social as well as emotional and physical) is endemic in modernity because the 'juggernaut' creates a sense of constant uncertainty. This uncertainty, Giddens argues, can constrain us to conform to social norms of safety such as 'be careful there's a big drop over that cliff', or it can empower us to explore, as in 'I wonder if I can climb up that cliff?'.

Structuration theory and the consequences of modernity

For Giddens (1990), the consequences of modernity are rooted in social institutions. The four dimensions that shape such organizational forms are capitalism, industrialism, military power and surveillance. The institutional dimension of the modern world raises important questions about how secure we feel in a world full of danger, who we trust and the nature of the risks that we confront collectively (e.g. nuclear war, global warming) and individually (e.g. is this part of town safe after dark?). It is the conditions of modernity that constantly de-stabilize our lives, threaten our sense of security and therefore affect our everyday practice. Yet, at the same time, such circumstances offer a plethora of lifestyle choices and opportunities. For Giddens (1982), practice means the ongoing processes of social interaction that generate our knowledge of the world:

> Neither the subject (human agent) nor the object ('society' or 'social institutions') should be regarded as having primacy. Each is constituted in and through recurrent practices. The notion of human 'action' presupposes that of 'institution' and vice versa. Explication of this relation thus comprises the core of an account of how it is that the structuration (production and re-production across time and space) of social practices takes place.
>
> *(p. 8)*

Practices exist across time and space because they are acknowledged and followed by most people in society. It is the everyday performance of practices that determine the extent to which 'structures' are reproduced or altered. So, the key idea here is that the production or re-production of behavioural practices at any given point in time occurs in relation to a set of rules that is determined by existing structures, such as economic determinants (e.g. class), which are established by historical precedents; it is the practices that establish the rules. At a structural level these rules are codified (e.g. wearing vibram-soled hiking footwear in the mountains) and operate as a framework of containment for our social behaviours. However, Giddens (1984) explains that some of the more trivial activities in daily life can have a profound effect on social conduct more generally. Rules, then, and how they are generated and enforced, can be formal or informal and are essential to the maintenance of social practices, and ultimately our sense of individual security (Giddens, 1991), which is maintained through the 'routinization' of social interactions. Such interactions allow us to communicate effectively, to exercise power and reflexively monitor, and therefore 'authorize', each other's actions.

According to Giddens (1984), rules become social *norms* and determine our core knowledge, which is then re-affirmed through social activity. Because they are socially determined, rules have the potential to be transformed over time, but this occurs in relation to power. Power operates throughout the social world in relation to resources. Resources give the means by which we can participate in different social settings. Giddens notes that resources can be *allocative* and *authoritative* (pp. 258–62). Allocative resources are the raw materials of social interaction; for a mountaineer this might mean possession of ropes, harnesses, climbing hardware and a means of transport to wild mountainous places. Authoritative resources refer to non-material resources and the capacity a person might have to control other people. An example might be a mountain guide who has a sanctioned status because of qualifications, specialist knowledge (such as details of the local mountain topology), reputation and experience.

In structuration theory, rules and resources combine to produce the social system (structure). Rules provide guidance by helping us interpret the core knowledge needed to navigate the choices encountered in everyday life. Resources shape this system by allowing certain people (who have access to greater resources) to control the behaviours of others. Giddens (1984) explains that informal rules combine with normative rules (which determine our rights and duties) to create 'practical consciousness' – the tacit (unspoken) ways of knowing how to behave in everyday life. This social system exists in a state of flux (because rules can be changed) yet provides continuity over time and space. Seen this way, 'structure is both the medium and the outcome of the practices it recursively organises' (Giddens, 1982, p. 10).

The relationship between individuals and institutions is therefore complex. This is because individuals and institutions are in constant interaction in the determination of everyday practices. Moreover, different institutions interact with each other (e.g. government and education or the Health and Safety Executive (HSE) and mountaineering). Structuration theory suggests that individuals access institutional structures to operate individual agency in different ways, as each of us is *positioned* differently in any particular set of social structures. Positioning both constrains and enables actions, but because there are differences in the distribution of know-ledge and resources in social systems, individuals are not situated in equal ways. Additionally, while we might be seen as knowledgeable actors, we are not necessarily fully aware of the implications of our actions, which may have unacknowledged conditions and unacknowledged consequences. British climbing, for example, originated from the activities of a small group of educated middle-class men who had the time and the means to travel to, and spend time in, the Lake District. This group undertook and recorded their ascents and developed the norms and rules for climbing because their social position made this possible.

This theoretical perspective, then, accommodates social dynamics, evolution and unpredictability, while recognizing the importance of continuity through routine. Routines are individually located and are typical of the life we lead and to which we are habituated, insofar as they reinforce our sense of everyday security. Routines are the foundations for self-esteem and thus our sense of identity (Giddens, 1991). Routines make us feel comfortable in the world, create a sense of purpose, moti-vation and order, and help to alleviate anxiety. A person who considers themselves a climber might routinely wear a climbing T-shirt at college, carry their books around in a small climbing rucksack and meet up regularly with friends at the local climbing wall/gym so that the identity of 'climber' is normalized by others who may or may not be climbers themselves. Routines are reflexively monitored by our practical consciousness (i.e. unconsciously) on an ongoing, everyday basis. However, when routines change, or we undertake patterns of behaviour that are not routine in the first place (such as signing up for a mountaineering trip abroad with an adventure tourism company), then we reflect on our actions in a conscious way that may lead to a new sense of identity (such as 'climber').

Clearly, this is a broad-ranging set of theoretical ideas, which, as many of the critical accounts of Giddens' work remind us, have very limited grounding in empirical investigation. Nevertheless, it is my contention that there is a wealth of potential application to the world of mountain-based adventure activities, and the following sections use mountaineering examples to highlight how Giddens' work contributes to an understanding of the sociology of adventure.

Mountaineering, institutions and power

At a macro level, and particularly (but not exclusively) in a British context, certain social groups (e.g. landowners and industrial interests such as forestry, mining and quarrying) control access to the wild places in which mountaineers operate. The famous class confrontation on Kinder Scout in the English Peak District in 1932 brought issues of *legitimation* to the fore (Donnelly, 1993). The working classes from the northern industrial cities of Sheffield and Manchester routinely used moorland walking as an escape from the drudgery of factory life, but found access to Kinder Scout denied by the gamekeepers that represented their employers (the landowners). The ensuing aggressive confrontation generated a court case that reaffirmed the rights of the landowners to close the moors to ramblers, in order to preserve the exclusivity of their grouse shooting rights. Although a 'Right to Roam' Act has now been passed by the British government, this imbalance in power still exists today as moors in the northern Peak District are still closed to hikers and climbers at certain times. The rules which determine access to mountain and moorland walking do therefore change, but still remain as a 'legitimate structure' that prioritizes shooting over walkers and demonstrates landowners exercising an 'authoritative' control (see also Chapter 13).

Routines form an essential part of how we locate ourselves in our everyday social lives. It has been suggested that the extent to which anyone might consider themselves to be a mountaineer can be thought of in terms of a sliding scale, with novice part-time mountaineers at one end and seasoned mountain guides at the other (Beedie, 2010). For novices, mountaineering is exceptional in their lives – outside everyday experience – and therefore the person will have limited understanding of the rules and norms of behaviour in that social setting. For mountain guides the opposite is the case, in that planning for and being in the mountains *is* their lives. There are differences in power between these extremes because of inequalities in the distribution of both allocative and authoritative resources. Mountain guides will endeavour to control 'their' mountain world (socially and spatially) by making sure that novice climbers are 'educated' into the correct way of participating in the sport.

In structuration theory, the dynamic of structure set against agency can have unintended consequences. In mountaineering, one of the ways government addressed the landowners/access to wild places issue was through the creation of national parks – a characteristic of social organization in the outdoors. While the intention was to increase access to wild and rugged landscapes for all, putting boundaries on a map has created social segregation. This circumstance is illustrated by Urry (1995) in his discussion of the 'making' of the English Lake District. He demonstrates that, although the policy-makers thought they were developing a collective 'good' in creating a park for all, because the powerful and influential middle classes identify closely with the value system of Romanticism, the Lake District has become a playground for the healthy and wealthy. Urry describes how a hiker whose journey took him to the declining industrial town of Cleator Moor in West Cumbria literally walked *out* of the Lake District. The culture shock of this juxtaposition is illustrated by the difference between the working-class and middle-class views of the West Cumbrian nuclear power station at Sellafield. This 'eyesore' (the aesthetic middle-class view) is clearly seen from the tops of many Lakeland fells, whereas the (utilitarian) view of the working-class locals recognizes that the power station represents a cleaner environment than the mining landscape it replaced and is an important source of local employment. So, not all social groups agree in the vision of a park for all, and such different perspectives raise the issue of identity as place specific.

Giddens (1984) suggests that social structures need to be reproduced, and if they are not, then their associated practices cease to exist. Since its inception in the nineteenth century, mountaineering in Britain has been organized through the club system, with the British Mountaineering Council (BMC) operating as a representative umbrella organization – rather like a national governing body in other sports. Originally, if a person wanted to become a mountaineer, he or she would join their local club. Senior club members could then promote the ethos, values and skill base associated with established mountaineering traditions, thus reinforcing certain patterns and practices within mountaineering. Typically, these practices demand a consolidation period (an apprenticeship), an appreciation of wild places through awe and reverence (in the Romantic tradition), and an understanding of constructing a mountaineering career through progression from crag climber to British hills to the Alps and then the greater ranges. As the social world changes, the reinforcement of these practices becomes less straightforward. Mountaineering clubs have less control over the ways in which ideas about the sport are circulated. Now that we have electronic media to bypass traditional conduits of practice reinforcement (e.g. websites, blogs and guidebooks that are not mountaineering-club endorsed), there is the possibility that mountaineering practices can be changed by people rather than simply being reinforced by them; not everyone who goes climbing today is a member of a BMC-affiliated climbing club, for example.

A particularly interesting application of structuration theory is the potential that social institutions have to contradict and undermine each other. For example, mountain guides operate as 'custodians' of the mountains (Collister, 1984), yet they guide people into the mountains, encourage independent mountaineering by giving their clients skills and knowledge, and thereby 'open the door' to mass infiltration of this delicate ecosystem of mountains. This is especially the case in British national parks, whereby the designation of these places as 'wild' acts like an 'adventure magnet' and threatens both the physical authenticity of wild mountains (e.g. by installing roads, paths, signposts and official camping grounds) and the social essence of mountaineering as 'solitudinous contemplation' in the Romantic tradition (Beedie, 2010).

A further example of this contradiction is the impact of guidebooks. When W.P. Haskett-Smith and Owen Glynne Jones published their British rock-climbing guidebooks at the turn of the twentieth century, the intention of separating mountain walkers from climbers (a point of distinction and consolidation of social status in the hierarchy of mountaineering) began. Through the designation of detailed rock-climbing grades a process of accelerated fragmentation within the sport emerged; for example, scrambling (a hybrid of climbing and walking) has developed as a mountaineering activity in its own right, with its own guidebooks and grading systems, and has caused the distinction between walkers and climbers to become blurred. Additionally, rather than generate a sense of completion as a mountain or climbing place reaches 'maturity' in terms of possible routes, guidebooks created challenges to climb harder. In Britain this circumstance became a class battleground as the working-class, city-based climbers, such as Manchester's Rock and Ice Club and Glasgow's 'Creagh-Dhu', challenged the existing middle-class cultural dominance in mountaineering mostly by climbing harder new routes that left guidebooks outdated almost as soon as they had been published.

Mountaineering, people, lifestyle and identity

Structuration theory suggests that social structures are located in individuals, but not necessarily in equal ways. Some people have greater access to knowledge and information than others, and various elements of the economy, family, media, culture and social environment combine to shape individual practices. As this environment changes, so too will social structures. The development of climbing walls demonstrates this point well. Climbing walls are artificial climbing structures that take many shapes and forms, are mostly static (a few are mobile towers) and, to varying degrees, 'mimic' a climbing experience. Climbing walls have been around since the 1960s, but, since these early examples were generally designed by architects (and not climbers), they were limited in their potential to simulate the 'real thing'. Walls are much more realistic today – principally due to the influence of entrepreneurial climbers keen to extend the idea of training for real mountaineering. Today, indoor climbing, because of its non-mountain location, has become a lifestyle choice for the many, as opposed to the realization of possibilities for the lucky few.

By significantly affecting the 'resource' dimension highlighted by structuration theory (time to climb and travel to wild places), technology and commercialization have combined to democratize access to mountaineering. As access to climbing has become more equal, challenges to traditional climbing and mountaineering identities are being mounted and social norms are being re-worked. Interestingly, in an act of resistance from mountaineering traditionalists, climbing walls use the French grading system (because the indoor routes are bolt protected). Furthermore, British sport climbing competitions are not permitted on real rock and are therefore restricted to climbing walls, which have spectating advantages and thus increased commercial potential. This example of the changing distribution of resources in the mountaineering world further illuminates the power struggles that an unequal distribution of resources generates.

There is now a new generation of climbers who have grown up at a time when there have always been climbing walls. This demonstrates a shift in the structures controlling access to climbing and mountaineering. In structuration theory terms, climbing walls have become an 'enablement' or a 'facility' of leisure preference that exists within a vast array of lifestyle choices. More than one structuring institution usually combines in this *facilitation*. For example, parents of novice adolescent climbers might endorse indoor walls over outdoor crags because they may be closer, safer and more controlled. Additionally, the peer group pressure of climbing-wall friends might encourage the use of climbing jargon and the display of climbing paraphernalia – both essential parts of identity construction.

Within structuration theory, facilitation becomes a concept useful for understanding the connection between the micro and the macro. This can be illustrated at a macro level by a short discussion about significant others in mountaineering. The records of mountaineering history show that when new conquests occur or climbing grades are advanced, the achievement is generally attached to a person. (Although I wrote 'person', this is sometimes 'people', as there is usually one person that benefits more – as did Maurice Herzog by being the author of *Annapurna*, which is an account of the French expedition that summitted the first 8,000m Himalayan giant in 1950, and is still the best-selling mountaineering book of all time.) Major climbing success brings social status and associated power and influence. There are still mountaineering 'firsts' being achieved today, which are facilitated by sophisticated global flows of specialist information, equipment and opportunities. In particular, the raised profile provided to climbing has attracted commercial and media attention such that today's Herzogs, Hillarys and Tilmans are becoming global celebrities. Celebrity status enables elite climbers to use their enhanced social profile to attract sponsorship of mountaineering essentials, such as equipment, food and clothing, in order for them to continue operating as professional mountaineers.

Mountaineering and change

With the fragmentation of mountaineering into niche activities, and the promotion of these in ways that diversify and divide the power base of traditional mountaineers, there was a clear change to the structuring dimensions of mountaineering. Today's media designate professional mountaineers as climbing celebrities, who commonly specialize in 'new' forms of mountaineering such as 'deep-water soloing' (climbing unroped on overhanging sea cliffs), Alpine ascents (a self-contained team of two climbers) of Himalayan 'giants' (traditionally climbed only with an army of climbers and supporting porters), big wall climbing in places that can only be accessed by water (such as some fjords in Greenland), and extreme sport climbing (involving outrageously hard moves with gymnastic precision on bolt-protected routes). Such celebrity climbers are usually young, strong, photogenic and suitably clad and equipped through sponsorship. Their images are used extensively for advertising climbing clothing, footwear, harnesses and other equipment in magazines and on the internet.

Lastly, in this very limited discussion of structuration theory and mountaineering, further reference needs to be made to Giddens' (1984) notion of *unforeseen consequences*. The history of mountaineering shows that, particularly in relation to exploration in the European Alps, which might be thought of as the symbolic birthplace of mountaineering, the visiting climbers (prominently British in the Golden Age of the mid-nineteenth century) relied upon the geographical knowledge and mountaineering expertise of local guides to facilitate their ascents. These guides were rarely given credit for the work they did, because there was a class difference between them and their employers (the rich Victorian mountaineers) and it was the educated mountaineers who wrote the books, which were the earliest broadcasting medium for the embryonic sport. The guides were, however, paid for their work, and this practice started the development of the mountain 'carnet' as the certification of expertise in mountain guiding and was overseen by a social organization that was to become the Union Internationale des Associations de Guides de Montagnes (UIAGM). Mountain guiding became a profession and, in a gradual loosening of the connections to aesthetics combined with an increasingly powerful concern about risk management, a structuring dimension of mountaineering. Although mountaineers might consider themselves to be custodians of wild places, this increasing momentum towards a business and commercial dimension has facilitated the development of adventure tourism. While there is not the space to discuss adventure tourism in any detail here, its growth (particularly mountain-based adventure tourism) has been rapid, and its operation is working against all that Romanticism in mountaineering represents, by increasing the forms of mountaineering (e.g. abseiling, bungy jumping, hang-gliding, via ferrata, gorge scrambling and canyoning) and the types and numbers of people who might consider themselves to be mountaineers.

Conclusions

Giddens' theoretical propositions can be usefully applied to illuminate the world of mountaineering. His concerns with security and identity formation lead to an understanding of mountaineering as a lifestyle choice. To choose to be a mountaineer engages two aspects of risk: the physical dangers of being in mountains and the social risks of presenting yourself in such a social setting. To become a mountaineer means to learn about the 'rules' that define the activity, and the extent to which these become routine norms is not fixed. Giddens' 'dialectic of control' is central to our reflexive 'radicalized' modern world and demonstrates how we are both constrained and empowered by the social conditions of our times. This is why mountaineering is dividing into sub-activities that are each influenced by the commercial provision of risk-managed environments (such as climbing walls, signposted walking paths and the development of adventure as business through tourism), and yet can still provide a much more adventurous platform for those people willing to seek out remote first ascents.

Globalization, and in particular the compression of time and space, has assisted the mobility of resources in ways that continue to fragment and diversify mountain activities. It is quite possible that a British-based climber might consider the granite crags of Joshua Tree national park in California as their climbing venue of choice. However, such structural 'freedoms' continue to operate alongside the 'constraints' of rules and norms for mountaineering. No one in Britain has yet drilled a bolt into the gritstone outcrops of the Peak District (bolted climbing is restricted to limestone crags), as climbing is still closely aligned to a set of commonly accepted ethics ('rules' originally outlined by the American climber Lito Tejeda-Flores in his seminal 1967 essay 'Games Climbers Play'), which represent the institutional traditions of the sport and serve to retain what climbers consider to be the essential challenge of adventure.

Further reading

For an introduction to applied social theory that explains Giddens' position on risk and security see Miles (2001) and then try Giddens (1999) himself in an accessible paper on the same theme.

Giddens, A. (1999) 'Risk and responsibility', *Modern Law Review*, 62(1), 1–10.
Miles, S. (2001) *Social theory in the real world*, London: Sage.

References

Beedie, P. (2010) *Mountain based adventure tourism: Lifestyle choice and identity formation*, Saarbrücken: Lambert Academic.
Collister, R. (1984) 'Adventure versus the mountain', *Alpine Journal*, 89, 123–5.
Donnelly, P. (1993) 'The right to wander: Issues in the leisure use of countryside and wilderness areas', *International Review for the Sociology of Sport*, 28(2), 187–200.
Giddens, A. (1982) *Profiles and critiques in social theory*, London: Macmillan Press.
Giddens, A. (1984) *The constitution of society: Outline of the theory of structuration*, Los Angeles: University of California Press.
Giddens, A. (1990) *The consequences of modernity*, Cambridge: Polity Press.
Giddens, A. (1991) *Modernity and self identity: Self and society in the late modern age*, Cambridge: Polity Press.
Stevenson, N. (2012) *Freedom*, London: Routledge.
Urry, J. (1995) *Consuming places*, London: Routledge.

10

MICHEL FOUCAULT

Power, surveillance and governmentality in outdoor education

Robyn Zink

This chapter focuses on the work of French philosopher, historian and social theorist Michel Foucault. A central tenet of Foucault's work is that there is nothing 'normal' or 'natural' about social practices; rather, what is seen as normal is so because of *normalizing* practices (Foucault, 2002a). Foucault used many different tools and strategies to investigate and analyse a wide range of social practices. Our discussion will use examples from a ropes course experience as a means of examining Foucault's notions of power, surveillance and governmentality.

Ropes courses, or challenge courses, have a military origin but were adapted in the 1970s to make the essence of Outward Bound courses more accessible. Ropes courses generally consist of a series of activities at ground level that have a focus on team-building and problem solving, as well as activities that are performed higher above the ground and have a greater emphasis on individual challenge and development (Prouty, 1999). This chapter starts with a brief description of Michel Foucault's life and then introduces some concepts that inform his thinking about power, surveillance and governmentality and are of relevance to our understanding of ropes courses and outdoor adventure more broadly.

Biography

Foucault was born in Poitiers, France, in 1924 to a well-to-do family. In 1952 he earned degrees in philosophy and psychology. From 1955 to 1959 he held various educational and diplomatic posts in Sweden, Germany and Poland, before returning to France, where he held a series of university posts. Foucault was elected to the Collège de France in 1969 at the relatively young age of forty-two. He held the position of Professor of the History of Systems of Thought until his death from AIDS in 1984. From 1979 he began to spend a significant amount of time working and teaching in northern California.

Foucault was politically very active. He formed the *Groupe d'information sur les prisons*, which advocated for penal reform, and he was an outspoken supporter of homosexuals and other marginalized groups. Naturally, Foucault's ideas continued to develop throughout his career, and his academic work became increasingly influenced by his political engagement (Veyne, 2010). He wrote on a wide range of subjects, including madness, the prison, the history of scientific thought and the history of sexuality. Towards the end of his life Foucault described the aim of his work as trying to uncover how human beings develop knowledge about themselves (Foucault, 2002c).

What Foucault's work has to offer outdoor adventure education

I am continually drawn to Foucault's work as it stimulates me to ask critical questions about outdoor education. As Grosz (2005) points out, the importance of philosophy and social theory is in the questions it prompts us to ask. She argues that, in many ways, the question or the problem is more significant than the solution. This is not to suggest that all we need to do is ask questions, but unless the question provokes us to think differently about something, the answer we find may only confirm what we already feel we know. Foucault saw his work as a tool bag for people to use in ways that were helpful to them. Next I discuss the ways in which Foucault conceived of practice, universalism and the subject, as these provide a context for understanding how he conceptualizes power, surveillance and governmentality.

Practice

Foucault had two starting points in his work. One was *practice*. Even though Foucault said his work was about uncovering how human beings develop knowledge about themselves, he focused on practice not the individual (Veyne, 2010). By practice he meant the 'places where what is said and what is done, rules imposed and reasons given, the planned and the taken-for-granted meet and interconnect' (Foucault, 2002a, p. 225). His aim was to understand the conditions that make a particular practice acceptable, or appear normal. Taking a Foucauldian approach involves trying to decipher what makes a ropes course experience seem like a good thing to do. Foucauldian-inspired questions might include an analysis of the taken-for-granted assumptions that lead teachers to believe that the things students can learn in a ropes course are relevant and important for the students. A teacher might choose a ropes course experience because it provides challenges for students with 'real' consequences, as they believe this delivers meaningful learning experiences that cannot be emulated in the classroom. This could lead to a series of questions about why particular types of experiences are thought to provide meaningful learning experiences and what this might tell us about the assumptions being made about learning and about young people.

Universalism

Foucault's second starting point was to 'suppose that universals simply do not exist' (Veyne, 2010, p. 17). For example, the statement that young people are risk-takers presumes that all young people share some universal behaviours and attributes. Foucault would argue that the assumption that all young people are risk-takers is a false concept that directs us to think about young people in particular ways. In starting from the point that universals do not exist, Foucault directs his questions at how a particular social practice comes to be seen as normal or 'real'. A Foucauldian analysis would look at how stories drawn from the military and Outward Bound are used in conjunction with the assumption that young people are risk-takers to make ropes courses seem like an obvious educational tool to use with young people. Walking across a pole suspended fifteen metres up in the air seems like a sensible thing to do because of the ways in which challenge and risk are privileged through military and Outward Bound narratives.

Foucault was interested in how practices come to be seen as natural or normalized, and he set out to *disqualify the natural object* (Veyne, 2010). By this he meant there is no point in seeking an 'objective' truth about a practice. In our outdoor education example, he would be much more interested in what makes ropes courses rational, legitimate and 'normal' today. While the ropes course experience might be the central focus of analysis, Foucault was not so much interested in the phenomenon itself; he was more interested in the *systematic relationships among elements*. For example, using a Foucauldian analysis, it is not possible to understand why a ropes course is seen as a good thing just by looking at what happens on a ropes course. We would need to examine the relationship between a ropes course and other educational institutions, such as schools and what we think is important for young people to learn. A student might say that she had learnt that she could do more than she thought she could after completing a high ropes course and this made her feel more confident. For those of us who have completed a ropes course this may seem like a natural outcome from this experience. But Foucault would argue that there is nothing inherent in a ropes course that makes increased confidence an automatic consequence of participation; we would need to look at the assumptions we make about ropes courses, education and young people to begin to understand why increased confidence is seen as a desirable outcome of this experience. In his work, Foucault was trying to uncover the systematic relationships that make practices meaningful at a given moment.

It is important to be clear that the relations of meaning that Foucault is looking for are very different from causal relations. He would not have been interested in the topic of how a ropes course experience, for example, might cause a change in self-esteem. Rather, he would be motivated to explore how ropes courses have come to be seen as an appropriate educational process, why self-esteem is seen as an important personal attribute, and why participating in something that is deemed challenging is thought to enhance self-esteem.

What we 'know' about what a ropes course 'does' is derived from its relationships to school-based education, from concepts of risk and adventure, from norms of how groups work together, and from broader economic discourses that frame the skills and attributes that young people should gain from education, to name but a few; what we know about a ropes course is not derived from something inherent within the ropes course itself. Meaning for Foucault is a relational concept, and meaning is tied to his concept of power. Before we move to a discussion of Foucault's concept of power, however, I will turn to how he conceived of the subject.

The subject

Just as Foucault did not believe that there was any essential meaning or truth inherent in a social practice, he did not hold that there was an essential 'self' either. That is, there is no 'natural' way to be a human being. Through detailed historical analysis, Foucault (2002c) traced how the knowledge human beings develop about themselves has changed. He saw the subject as a form, rather than a substance.

In the ropes course, students' behaviour and the way they make sense of their experiences are not due to their innate personalities or characteristics. Rather, their behaviour is formed by the social world they inhabit. Even though students that I have worked with on ropes courses consistently comment that they feel more confident after the activity, Foucault would argue that this is because we live in a world where it is seen as good to be confident, not because of any innate human characteristic or trait. Foucauldian-inspired questions in this situation might focus on how it is possible to be a student in this context, what counts as a good/bad student, and how this is shaped by the relations of meaning that make a ropes course seem a sensible educational response to what are perceived as the needs of young people. I now turn to three of Foucault's analytical tools: power, surveillance and governmentality.

Power

Foucault theorizes relations of power in quite a different way from structuralists such as Marx, who saw power being held by a few at the top and exercised on the many below. For Foucault (1995), power produces reality; it is the productive capacities of power that make it acceptable and even desirable (Foucault, 2002c). Foucault was not so much interested in power itself, but in how *relations of power* work both to produce and to repress possibilities of human thought and action.

Relations of power produce what can be known about something (the 'truth'), and what is silenced about a practice. By truth, Foucault is not implying that the 'real' meaning of an object or practice can be discerned. When he talks about truth, he is referring to truth 'games', which are 'a set of rules by which truth is produced' (Foucault, 2000, p. 297), and how a practice comes to make sense. A Foucauldian approach requires us to question how 'what is' thought to be *true* about rope course practices comes to be seen as true. This points to a power/truth complex. This does not mean that truth is at the mercy of power, but that there is an intricate relationship between the two. What we 'know' about the ropes course informs what we do in the ropes course, which in turn shapes what we know about the ropes course. For example, we 'know' that young people learn by doing things that are out of their comfort zone; therefore we encourage them to challenge themselves to do more than they thought they could, which leads to developing activities in the ropes course that challenge participants in particular ways. Foucault-inspired questions might focus on what is being said about how young people learn and how this influences the design of ropes course programmes.

Foucault (2000) notes that there is no objective point from which to measure the veracity or effectiveness of a practice. Rather, particular ways of operating emerge as 'correct' or 'appropriate' through complexes of truth and power (Foucault, 2000). These complexes are not fixed, as evidenced by moves from activity- and pursuits-based pedagogies towards place-based pedagogies in some contexts (Wattchow and Brown, 2011). In examining truth games, Foucault (2000) is not suggesting that a practice is 'wrong'; he is highlighting that a particular practice is not necessarily the 'only' response to contemporary issues. Foucault would not suggest that a student who claims to have gained in confidence by doing the ropes course is misguided or deluded in that claim. He would be more interested in understanding why confidence is seen as important at this time, and how this shapes the learning experiences we design for students.

One of the critiques of Foucault's work is that it leads to *relativism*, or that anything goes because nothing is fixed to an objective or permanent point. But Foucault argues that while truth is not fixed to an objective point, a practice has to make sense within the context or time. Ropes courses make sense *now* because of how we understand the needs of young people. If we were to choose to do some other activity, we could not just choose any activity; we could only choose an activity that makes sense in relation to what we understand as the needs of young people today. Veyne (2010) explains this notion of truths and practices not being fixed by highlighting how in

> every age, contemporaries are thus trapped in 'discourses' as if in a deceptively transparent glass bowl, unaware of what those glass bowls are and even that they are there. False generalities and 'discourses' vary from age to age. But in every period they are taken to be true. In this way, truth is reduced to *telling the truth*, to saying whatever conforms with what is accepted as the truth, even though this will make people smile a century later.
>
> (*p. 14, original emphasis*)

We may smile now that outdoor education was seen as inappropriate for girls as little as fifty years ago (Cook, 2001), but at the time that would have been a self-evident truth. Power relations produce 'truth' and they also direct human behaviour and produce subjects, and we now turn to the disciplinary function of power.

Discipline

Foucault was interested in the techniques and procedures for directing human behaviour. In *Discipline and Punish: The Birth of the Prison*, Foucault (1995) argued that: 'Discipline "makes" individuals; it is the specific technique of a power that regards individuals both as objects and instruments of its exercise' (p. 170). Discipline is not a 'triumphant power' that rules over everyone with the aim of reducing 'all its subjects into a single uniform mass' (p. 170). Foucault described disciplinary power as subtle in the way it influences individuals. The practice of groups setting ground rules or group contracts at the beginning of a ropes course session is an example of this subtle operation of power. Setting the ground rules is one of the many elements of early group life that contribute to the 'culture' of the group and to establishing its norms of behaviour. A Foucauldian analysis shifts from questions of who holds the power in this situation to questions of how ground rules established by the group make certain behaviours and actions acceptable, and in turn how students can develop knowledge about themselves in this context.

Individuals within the group are objects of those rules, in that their behaviour is influenced by those rules. They are also instruments of those rules, in that each person participates in setting the ground rules and everyone in the group monitors their own behaviour and the behaviour of others in relation to those rules. But this is a variable process. Not everyone will have the same influence in determining the ground rules. The instructor will have greater influence on the ground rules than students. This influence can be overt, if they state what acceptable ground rules are, or it can be subtle, with a nod of the head for approval when a 'good' ground rule is suggested. Participants will also have variable influences on determining ground rules. Foucault-inspired questions might centre on whose voices dominate when establishing the ground rules and what norms become established within a group. Again, this type of analysis requires the researcher to look beyond the site of the ropes course and consider the normalizing practices in broader educational and social contexts that make specific practices within the ropes course appear to be good or acceptable.

Relationships of power are always at work and are both productive and repressive. While Foucault certainly recognized that relations of domination or triumphant power existed, he was more interested in the subtle operations of power. The following section describes some of the ways in which we are all implicated in relations of power.

Surveillance

One common feature of contemporary society is the surveillance of individuals. Jeremy Bentham's *Panopticon* is the architectural model of how this surveillance occurs. Designed as a prison, the Panopticon is shaped like a ring, with cells lining the periphery of the building and, in the centre, a tower with wide windows facing the cells. Each cell houses one person, who cannot see or communicate with any one else. In the tower is a guard who can see the inmates but is not seen by them. The ingenuity of the Panopticon is that the inmates never know when they are being observed; hence it arranges 'things [so] that the surveillance is permanent in its effects, even if it is discontinuous in its action' (Foucault, 1995, p. 201). The inmates act as if they are being constantly observed, even when there is no one watching them.

The power of surveillance does not sit with the guard or the institution. Because the prisoners act as if they are under permanent surveillance (that is, they monitor and regulate their own behaviour), they are enmeshed in the power relations that create their understanding of themselves and of their behaviour; they are effectively doing surveillance on themselves. The Panopticon model can be used in any situation where many people are required to behave in similar ways, as in schools. It is a 'type of power' (Foucault, 1995, p. 215) or a technology of power, rather than being a force belonging to an institution.

The architecture of the Panopticon could not be further from the architecture of the spaces in which outdoor education usually occurs. After all, there are literally no walls in this space. But the type of power that operates in the Panopticon operates equally well in outdoor environments. In the case of the group contract which lays out the norms of group behaviour, its effectiveness is not due to everyone signing this agreement and behaviour being monitored in a deliberate manner by the instructor. The effectiveness of the group contract is that students monitor their own behaviour, even when the instructor is not looking. We become enmeshed in these relations of power because, as Foucault (1995) writes, the aim of surveillance is to strengthen social forces, not just to repress or dominate (p. 208). The logic of a group contract is to facilitate productive group relationships and to enable a group to achieve its aims. Questions a researcher might ask are: what sorts of behaviours does a group contract support, why are these particular behaviours thought to facilitate productive group relationships, and how does it direct human behaviour?

Dividing practices

Foucault (1995) identified three instruments that contribute to the success of surveillance in 'making' individuals. These are what he termed the dividing practices of hierarchical observation, normalizing judgement and the examination. *Hierarchical observation* relates to how surveillance occurs from the top down and from the bottom up. But, as Foucault notes, this instrument of surveillance is discreet because, while it works on the individual, it works through a whole network of relationships. In educational settings, this type of surveillance 'is at the heart of the practice of teaching, not as an additional or adjacent part, but as a mechanism that is inherent to it and which increases its efficiency' (Foucault, 1995, p. 176). An example of top-down observation is an instructor grading students on their participation. This stands in contrast to the reflection processes that are part of many ropes course programmes, which can be characterized as bottom–up hierarchical observation, where students subtly observe each other. Going around the circle in the debrief is at the heart of the learning process in the ropes course; it is part of the whole network of relationships that makes a ropes course meaningful. When going around the circle students not only talk about their experience, they also listen to others and make assessments about where their experiences fit in the group. This illustrates how discreet surveillance is because it is integral to what happens in a ropes course. Key questions to consider are: how do hierarchical observations work, and how does this shape our practice?

Normalizing judgements work to define behaviour and performance on the basis of 'good' and 'bad'. Individuals are differentiated based on where their behaviour falls between these poles of good and bad. But Foucault argues it is not just the behaviour that is marked as good or bad; the individual is also labelled as good or bad and thus differentiated from others by their position between these poles. In short, normalizing judgements measure subjects in relation to each other and introduce 'all the shading of individual differences' (Foucault, 1995, p. 184). A Foucauldian analysis would not focus on where a student falls between these poles. Instead, the analysis would focus on how behaviour is characterized as good and bad, how these labels are fixed to subjects, and the effect this has on the way a ropes course programme is organized. For example, in assessing leadership, rather than matching student behaviour against a set of criteria, the analysis would start by asking why 'these' criteria are being used, how these particular ideas about leadership have come to be seen as 'right' in this context, and how this shapes the ways in which students see themselves as leaders.

Examination is the third instrument of Foucault's dividing practices. It combines hierarchical observation and normalizing judgements into a 'gaze', which in turn makes individuals 'visible'. Two things are at work in the instrument of examination. First, the individual is constituted as describable and analysable. Second, a system of comparison is created. Foucault (1995, p. 192) argued that the examination was a new form of power that pins down 'each individual in his [*sic*] own particularity . . . in which each individual receives as his status his own individuality'. We live in an age where every form of behaviour has, at a minimum, a label, if not a pathology, attached to it. Instructors constantly describe and analyse students, and students also describe and analyse their peers, and themselves. Reflection processes often require students to determine how they think they did, compare that to how they thought they would do, and consider what they would do differently next time.

The dividing practices work together to 'produce' the individual – to measure and classify them, and to rank them in relation to other individuals. Inevitably, the focus in these individualizing processes falls on the 'non-norm', or on those people who do not fit or comply within accepted truths of what is normal, right or good. For example, the 'delinquent' youth is of greater interest than the 'normal' student. Working with Foucault, researchers do not set out to understand the phenomenon that is the non-norm, but instead explore the relationships between what counts as the norm and the non-norm and how these relationships constitute particular practices and subjects.

Governmentality

Discipline and surveillance target the individual. Governmentality targets the population. Foucault turned to governmentality as a means of exploring the practices of governing the state and the self that developed in the West after feudalism. He argued that the focus of the modern state is on the administration of populations (Foucault, 2002b). As with all of his work, in his studies of governmentality Foucault was interested in the question of how power works. Governmentality examines how populations are organized and managed through institutions such as education, health and the economy. A Foucauldian might argue that the ropes course is a popular educational tool as it delivers an outdoor learning experience more efficiently than other outdoor activities can, not because it necessarily provides a superior outdoor learning experience.

Governmentality cannot be understood outside of neo-liberalism and the market economy today. Foucault (2002b) argued that what distinguishes modern modes of governing in the West from earlier times is that the state does not rely on triumphant power. The state relies on people being able to organize themselves and take responsibility for their decisions and actions, and this is framed through the rule of the market economy, privatization and deregulation. There is substantial criticism of neo-liberalism and the ways it shapes how it is possible to understand ourselves as human beings and much of this literature draws on the work of Foucault (see, for example, Besley and Peters, 2007).

In the West, the idea that individuals make their own decisions about what is in their best interest and take responsibility for those decisions is so normalized that we often find it difficult to imagine there is any other way in which we might wish to organize ourselves. Had Foucault become interested in the practices of outdoor education, he might have investigated how common learning objectives in ropes courses reflect or support the idea that young people need to learn how to make decisions and take responsibility for those decisions. Analysis of this type might draw attention to concepts such as challenge-by-choice where students identify the level of challenge they choose to take on and make a commitment to achieve the desired outcome. Challenge-by-choice 'works' because it enables instructors and students to develop knowledge about themselves that equips them to function in ways required for them to be successful in the modern state; that is, to take responsibility for the decisions they make.

As noted earlier, when examining truth games, Foucault was not setting out to prove a practice was wrong. He was trying to uncover the assumptions that make something like a ropes course seem like a good thing to do at this point in time. His project was to uncover how human beings develop knowledge about themselves, and his analysis of the ropes course would revolve around this key question. By focusing on the practices that occur within the ropes course, not the individual student, a Foucauldian-inspired analysis has to take account of the social world in which the practice of the ropes course makes sense. This analysis explores the systematic relationships between education, adventure, the economic environment and our ideas about young people and how these relations work together to make ropes courses seem like a sensible educational experience today.

Another note on power

Veyne (2010) reminds us that we cannot escape relations of power; power is everywhere. When first reading about disciplinary modes of power, the ways in which surveillance and dividing practices produce individuals may appear repressive and possibly negative (Foucault, 1995). While Foucault did not deny that power can be repressive, he also argued that power is productive. As noted above, power works because it aims to strengthen social forces. An example of 'productive' power is provided by the myriad ways in which surveillance can produce a supportive group culture that enables individuals to interact with each other in a way that would otherwise not be possible.

Unlike Marx, Foucault did not view the operations of power on the subject as tricking or duping an individual into behaving in a particular way, in order to meet the objectives of a larger 'power'. He would not have regarded a group that develops ground rules for their time together as being trapped in a state of false consciousness (see Chapter 2), where they think they have set the rules but are essentially governed by someone else. Foucault did not set out to find a 'true' or 'real' human nature that had become concealed by social or cultural processes. He was interested in how we come to understand ourselves as human beings through the social world we inhabit, and how we can fashion ourselves within that social world (Foucault, 2000).

Conclusion

Foucault argues that the individual is messy, complex and contradictory. Thus, the focus of Foucault-inspired work foregrounds students' experiences of outdoor education in a very different way from research that endeavours to measure pre-determined personal traits or attributes that are thought to tell us something about the development and learning of young people. Foucault helps us shift our focus to the ways in which young people fashion themselves as students within the social world they inhabit and towards the meanings they derive from the practices and relations of power in which they are located (Foucault, 2002c).

Foucault was trying to describe how the 'glass bowl' of our time works (Veyne, 2010). A starting point when using Foucault's tools is the taken-for-granted assumptions that underpin outdoor education practices. To do this type of analysis, the phenomenon of outdoor education has to be located in its social and historical context. Practices are messy and contradictory, in the same way that subjects are messy and contradictory. This mess and contradiction can make it a challenge to find a coherent story to tell about the practice of outdoor education, but can also provide a rich context for prompting us to think differently as we struggle to understand its complexities.

Further reading

Bowdridge, M. and Blenkinsop, S. (2008) 'Michel Foucault goes outside: Discipline and control in the practice of outdoor education', *Journal of Experiential Education*, 34(2), 149–63.

Foucault, M. (2002) 'The subject and power', in J.D. Faubion (ed.), *Essential works of Foucault 1954–1984: Power* (vol. 3, pp. 326–48), London: Penguin.

References

Besley, A.C. (Tina) and Peters, M.A. (2007) *Subjectivity and truth: Foucault, education and the culture of the self*, New York: Peter Lang.

Cook, L. (2001) 'Differential social and political influences on girls and boys through education out of doors in the United Kingdom', *Journal of Adventure Education and Outdoor Learning*, 1(2), 43–52.

Foucault, M. (1995) *Discipline and punish: The birth of the prison*, trans. A. Sheridan, New York: Vintage.

Foucault, M. (2000) 'The ethics of the concern for self as a practice of freedom', in P. Rabinow (ed.), *Essential works of Foucault 1954–1984: Ethics, subjectivity and truth* (vol. 1, pp. 281–301), London: Penguin.

Foucault, M. (2002a) 'Questions of method', in J.D. Faubion (ed.), *Essential works of Foucault 1954–1984: Power* (vol. 3, pp. 223–38), London: Penguin.

Foucault, M. (2002b) 'Governmentality', in J.D. Faubion (ed.), *Essential works of Foucault 1954–1984: Power* (vol. 3, pp. 201–22), London: Penguin.

Foucault, M. (2002c) 'The subject and power', in J.D. Faubion (ed.), *Essential works of Foucault 1954–1984: Power* (vol. 3, pp. 326–48), London: Penguin.

Grosz, E. (2005) *Time travels: Feminism, nature, power*, Crows Nest, Australia: Allen & Unwin.

Prouty, D. (1999) 'Project adventure: A brief history', in J.C. Miles and S. Priest (eds), *Adventure programming* (pp. 93–101), State College, PA: Venture.

Veyne, P. (2010) *Foucault: His thought, his character*, trans. J. Lloyd, Cambridge: Polity Press.

Wattchow, B. and Brown, M. (2011) *A pedagogy of place: Outdoor education for a changing world*, Clayton, Australia: Monash University.

PART III

Contemporary themes in social theory and adventurous activities

11

FEMINIST THEORY AND OUTDOOR LEADERSHIP

Linda Allin and Amanda West

Introduction

This chapter focuses on feminist theory and its application to outdoor leadership. In it, we challenge popular conceptions and misconceptions about feminism (or, more correctly, *feminisms*) and aim to develop a basic understanding of feminist theory. We begin by providing some historical background to feminism before outlining some broad feminist perspectives, namely: liberal, radical, socialist and post-structural feminism. As we work through these different feminist perspectives, we show how each can be used to inform an analysis of gender in relation to outdoor instructor qualification schemes and outdoor leadership.

First, second and third wave feminism

Popular conceptions of feminism and feminists invoke an image of groups of strident women with little sense of humour (they just don't get sexist jokes), agitating for power and ill-disposed to men. At best, feminists pose a threat to the status quo and at worst they seek to overthrow traditional gender roles, which can lead to the breakdown of society. Indeed, this was exactly how David Lloyd George's coalition government viewed the *first wave feminists* – the Suffragettes who demanded the vote in the early twentieth century. Women having secured the vote and accrued some rights to property and divorce, *second wave feminism* emerged in the 1960s and 1970s as part of the general Civil Rights movement, demanding, among other things, equal pay for work of equal value. Second wave feminism challenged men's privileged position in the public sphere of life (civil society and the work place) and women's undervalued position in the private sphere of life (the home and family).

The apparent strength of second wave feminism was its coalescence around womanhood. However, this had become a source of weakness by the 1990s.

Powerful critiques by black feminists challenged the assumption that women's experiences were sufficiently similar to warrant a single approach to tackling gender inequality. They pointed out that, for some women, racism acts as a more powerful source of oppression than sexism. In response to a growing realization that women's experiences are multiple rather than singular, *third wave feminism* emerged and recognized the diversity of women's experiences.

Although there have been different waves of feminism and contrasting theoretical approaches, a commonality in feminist research is an attempt to enhance understanding of women's lives and to challenge gender inequality. In this chapter, we explore questions about gender in relation to outdoor leadership, and consider the solutions different feminist perspectives offer to enhance women's experiences of outdoor leadership schemes.

Liberal feminism

A key concern for liberal feminists is the belief that women should have equal rights with men. Liberal feminists believe that gender differences are not rooted in biology, and that men and women are more similar than different. All individuals, therefore, should have equal status under the law and the same opportunities in education and work. A key concept for liberal feminists is *equality of opportunity* and the recognition of individual talent. The liberal principle behind equal opportunities is therefore to remove collective and discriminatory barriers that prevent, in work, the 'best person' being appointed to jobs. Key liberal feminists advocating women's rights have been Mary Wollstonecraft (eighteenth century), Betty Friedan and Gloria Steinem (twentieth century).

Liberal feminists frequently cite evidence of inequalities by referring to the number of men and women in different occupational roles. For example, male employees are most likely to be working as managers and senior officials, and least likely to be working in administrative and secretarial, sales and customer services and personal services occupations. The opposite is true for women (ONS, 2009). In sport, women make up only 22 per cent of board members of governing body associations and are highly under-represented in the senior administrator positions (Women's Sport and Fitness Foundation, 2012). Although very little data are available about the number of women in outdoor leadership roles, the data that do exist suggest that women are under-represented compared to men as outdoor instructors, particularly at the highest levels (Sharp, 2001). Examination of the 2012 members list of the British Mountain Guides also shows that out of approximately 190 mountain guides, only seven (under 4 per cent) are women.

For liberal feminists, inequalities between men and women arise through processes such as gendered socialization and the gendered division of labour, which favour men. Gendered socialization refers to the way in which boys and girls learn social norms and expectations according to their sex and hence learn their gender identities. This occurs through both formal and informal processes, via key socializing agents such as the family, peers and teachers, and institutions such as the home, school and work. Gender socialization begins very early on in life and is typically based on and reinforces stereotypical thinking. For example, girls are more often directed by parents towards playing passively with dolls, whereas boys are taught to play with cars or guns, while being active and in charge. Learning that there are differential interests by sex can be reinforced through gender stereotypical images in books or differentiating tasks at school. Later on, peer pressure and the activities of different friendship groups often move girls away from any engagement in physical activity and sport. At home, girls may be more encouraged to play indoors or near the house, while boys may be more likely to be encouraged to play outdoors in rough and tumble activities. What is evident is that from early to middle childhood boys spend more time in active play outdoors in their leisure time, and girls spend more time indoors (Cherney and London, 2006). The implication for outdoor leadership is that girls and young women experience fewer opportunities to develop skills and confidence in outdoor environments prior to becoming an outdoor leader. Unintentionally, this also means women are less likely to pursue careers as outdoor leaders.

The gendered division of labour describes the extent to which women and men do different types of work and the way in which 'women's work' is devalued. For example, in developed countries, men are more likely to be engaged in physical, technical or senior professional work, while women are more likely to be engaged in domestic or caring work. In relation to outdoor leadership, the gendered division of labour would refer to women outdoor leaders being more likely to facilitate social skills than be engaged in technically focused work, or women leaders being more likely to work with younger and less experienced clients. While there are little data as to whether this happens in outdoor leadership, research about women's experiences as sports coaches indicates that they perceive themselves as less likely to coach male performers or performers at the highest levels and more likely than male coaches to coach children or novice performers (West et al., 2001). Liberal feminists also note that women are more likely to experience the 'glass ceiling effect' in their careers, whereby they are restricted from reaching the top occupational positions by hidden discriminatory practices. Again, little research exists in respect to outdoor leadership, but West et al. (2001) found that women sports coaches reported difficulty accessing high-level sports coaching roles, citing closed social networks as one reason.

Similar practices may include gender stereotypical beliefs by managers or hiring practices that inadvertently disadvantage women. Discriminatory practices may occur in the outdoors when higher level outdoor managers perceive women leaders as more suitable for particular roles than others, or where jobs arise through 'old boys'' networks – informal male social networks to which women have less access. Indeed, Loeffler (1995), writing from North America, cited the exclusion of women from these networks as a key barrier to women's progression in outdoor leadership. The lack of role models for women in higher outdoor leadership positions may also lead women to believe that these roles are not achievable for them.

For liberal feminists, equality is sought through recourse to the law and through lobbying. Specific liberal feminist actions include the promotion of non-sexist education and non-sexist media representation. Two important pieces of legislation in the UK addressing discriminatory practices have been the Equal Pay Act (1970) and the Sex Discrimination Act (1975). Both of these have now been subsumed by the Equality Act (2010) and have made a considerable difference to women's achievements in society and in the outdoors. Celebrating women's successes and raising awareness of women's contributions in society and the outdoors have also accelerated the drive towards gender equality. Typical strategies to encourage the number of women outdoor leaders from this perspective have included raising women's visibility through successful role models, challenging stereotypes about women's lack of physical or technical competence, and enhancing women's opportunities to acquire the necessary skills (Saunders and Sharp, 2002; Warren and Loeffler, 2006).

Liberal feminists would advocate visible female instructors or co-instructors on training and assessment courses, with women taking an equal part with men in such activities as leadership decision-making, unloading the minibus and mentoring participants. Women may also benefit from additional opportunities to support their technical skill development and confidence in areas such as map reading. This might include active strategies to encourage women to participate in skill development courses. This latter point reflects liberal feminist calls for women to be offered increased or different opportunities where necessary, in order to support their involvement and progression. Such strategies can play a role in enhancing women's involvement in outdoor instruction and leadership, and can be seen in many outdoor organizations' or governing body's equal opportunities literature, policies and strategies. For example, the UK Royal Yachting Association (RYA) (2009) 'Equality Action Plan 2009–13' includes a commitment to investigating barriers to women undertaking RYA coaching courses and targeting women with positive interventions.

However, liberal feminist approaches have been criticized for the way they position women as the problem which needs a solution, rather than challenging the structures which can disadvantage women in the first instance. That is, this perspective does not involve any critique of the content or structure of outdoor qualification or progression systems themselves, the ways in which 'good leadership' is defined, or the fact that most outdoor assessors and designers of outdoor qualification systems at the higher levels are male. The weakness of liberal feminism is therefore that it assumes legislation and formal frameworks will guarantee opportunities for women, and that equal access to opportunities will lead to equal outcomes in terms of progression in jobs or qualifications. It ignores the capacity of those with a vested interest in retaining the status quo to resist change.

Radical feminism

While liberal feminism focuses on addressing the causes of women's equality in public life, radical feminism begins by tackling women's position in the home, or the private sphere of life. Radical feminists argue that the cause of a woman's unequal position in society is male control over her body, particularly with respect to her sexuality as the bearer of children, but also in terms of her physical appearance.

For radical feminists, a key concept in understanding gender inequality is that of *patriarchy*. Patriarchy, or literally 'rule of the father', initially referred to the power of the male head of the household over females and younger males, but is now used more broadly within feminist work to describe a societal-wide system of gender social power relations, where men dominate women. Radical feminists accept biological differences between men and women, and indeed some celebrate such differences by emphasizing women's closeness to nature and relationships, due to their involvement in child-bearing and child-rearing. Feminists such as Adrienne Rich (1977), for example, advocated the position that the process of motherhood allowed women to see the world in a different, more connected way than men.

Explanations for women's subordination, from a radical feminist viewpoint, are based either on male biology – their natural aggression which they use to dominate women – or on the meaning attached to biological differences, such as the ways in which women's experiences or strengths or roles have been devalued. For example, radical feminism would highlight differences between men and women outdoor leaders in the possession and valuation of technical 'hard' skills versus inter-personal 'soft' skills. One research study with outdoor instructors has shown that men express greater confidence about their technical ability and value it more highly than women (Sharp, 2001). Conversely, women tend to value knowledge-based activities such as planning and preparation. Such reported differences reflect and reinforce radical feminist essentialist arguments about supposed natural differences between men and women. In terms of outdoor leadership, radical feminist approaches would critique 'male' models of outdoor leadership that encourage physicality, authoritarianism, competitiveness or aggression, and replace them with more 'female' approaches or styles that emphasize co-operation, consensus and communication.

Radical feminists would also highlight the use of sexist and sexualized language by outdoor leaders, which serves to reinforce male superiority. For example, the term 'shuttle bunny' is taken from the corseted waitresses the 'Playboy Bunnies' and used to refer to the person in the group (traditionally female) who is not kayaking the river, but is there to drive those who are (traditionally male) to the top of the river and then collect them at the bottom. Moreover, the imperative for women to look good (for men) exists even in the outdoors (Haluza-DeLay and Dyment, 2003; McDermott, 2004). This involves maintaining a heterosexual personal appearance, perhaps by paying particular attention to hair, dress or accessories, or else risking being labelled 'lesbian' (Loeffler, 1995).

Women's competence can also be undermined by male chauvinism on outdoor courses. For example, Allin (2000) reported the experiences of some women in her study who explained how, on a predominantly male instructor course, a man's cry of 'do you really think you can handle a force five?' or 'phew, it's hairy out there, are you sure you want to be going out?' can undermine women's confidence despite their ability (p. 59). The existence of both sexualized and chauvinistic behaviour acts as a potential distraction from women's roles as outdoor practitioners, while undermining their perceived status among male outdoor leaders who may judge their sexuality before their competence.

The radicalism in radical feminism lies in the solution offered to address the male-dominated and 'masculine' approach to outdoor leadership and instruction, which is for women to claim a women-only space and free themselves from patriarchal power (male oppression). Such views found expression in the 1970s in particular through women-only communes. In the outdoors, Henderson (1996) identifies how this approach is evident in the North American group Woodswomen, Inc., which applies a 'feminist transformational leadership' model to its work. She draws from Mitten (1992, p. 58) to show how this group emphasizes the provision of empowering outdoor experiences through principles such as being supportive, creating an emotionally and physically safe space for women, travelling in the wilderness for its own sake and viewing leadership as a relationship and not a personality type.

Broader support for separatism among outdoor leaders is more equivocal. Survey responses from a sample of 258 male and female instructors indicated a strong preference for maintaining the existing content of courses. However, there was some support for the provision of women-only courses in the early stages of skill development and leadership training, to develop confidence (Saunders and Sharp, 2002). Other studies have also demonstrated the potential value of women-only training courses in developing technical skills and building confidence in a supportive atmosphere (Warren, 1996; Hornibrook et al., 1997; McDermott, 2004). UK outdoor governing bodies such as the British Canoe Union have introduced with some success women-only courses as one of their strategies to increase women's participation and entry to outdoor qualifications. Saunders and Sharp (2002), however, warn that women-only courses may be viewed by some as being of a lower standard and thus attract less qualified applicants. That such a thought would occur to both men and women in itself reflects gendered assumptions about the inferiority of women's abilities in relation to those of men. It also supports liberal feminist views of the neutrality of the 'standard' by which male and female leaders are judged. Radical feminists would challenge this neutrality. For example, they would question the need for some of the physical endurance elements within some higher level outdoor qualification schemes. They would highlight an overemphasis on physicality as an exclusionary strategy aimed at reinforcing male physical dominance and their 'natural' position as leaders.

Critics of radical feminism assert that the concept of patriarchy is too ill-defined to provide a satisfactory explanation for gender inequality. That is, the notion of patriarchy, or 'male rule', is a universal one that implies that all men dominate all women. This does not account for the different experiences of women or indeed of men. Moreover, radical feminism views men and women as essentially different (innately and inherently) and consequently overlooks the shared experiences of men and women, and their capacity to behave in similar ways. This essentialism ignores the very many differences that exist between women, such as social class, race, sexual orientation and disability.

Socialist feminism

Socialist feminists argue that women's oppression is a consequence of both patriarchy and capitalism. That is, they acknowledge the existence of patriarchal relations but suggest that patriarchy alone is insufficient to explain women's unequal position in society and that an analysis of capitalism to understand women's unequal position is needed. The most well-known theorist associated with the concept of capitalism is Karl Marx. As we saw in Chapter 2, for Marx, capitalism is an economic and social system where the means of producing and distributing goods are owned by a minority (employers) and the majority (workers) labour for a wage paid by employers. By failing to pass on the full value of workers' labour, employers profit from (and exploit, Marx would argue) the majority for personal gain.

When applying a Marxist analysis to the home setting, socialist feminists propose that women are engaged in reproductive labour, which means that their work has no exchange value. Women therefore labour for free in the home and for the family. This arrangement benefits men and enables them to participate in productive labour, as well as leisure activities (Thompson, 1999). In terms of understanding outdoor leadership schemes and progression, it can be argued that women's work in the home makes it more difficult for them to afford either the money or the time to engage in instructor courses or develop outdoor expertise, particularly as most schemes require recorded evidence of leadership and personal experience as a pre-requisite for entry.

While the pattern of women's and men's employment is changing, even when women are at work, evidence suggests that women are still responsible for the majority of childcare and domestic chores. Moreover, women tend to fit leisure around childcare responsibilities and often feel guilty about taking time 'for themselves' (Deem, 1986; Allin, 2003). Allin's study also showed that many women following careers in the outdoors found themselves becoming de-skilled, as it was difficult to continue to develop outdoor qualifications and skills due to family responsibilities, particularly when their children were young. Long and unsociable hours for work or qualification courses further exacerbate the issue. For example, working at an outdoor centre can require evening and weekend work, plus extended periods of time away on expeditions. For women with children, there are con-siderable practical and financial issues associated with arranging childcare for such erratic hours. Without a very strong social network or financial background, finding additional time and resources to take part in qualification courses or consolidate personal outdoor skills can be very difficult. This situation supports both patriarchy and capitalism at the expense of gender equality in both the home and the workplace. Solutions to these circumstances involve addressing and changing women's financial and material conditions, most notably in relation to childcare.

Despite efforts to construct a more nuanced analysis of patriarchy that considers social class differences (Walby, 1990), socialist feminism's reliance on the ill-defined concept of patriarchy is one of its key weaknesses. Its failure to acknowledge the diversity of women's experiences beyond those of social class is a second. Finally, a third criticism of socialist feminism is that in countries which embrace(d) socialism there is little to suggest that women enjoyed a more equal position than men.

Post-structural feminism

The post-structuralist project led to a radical re-interpretation of social life and challenged, for example, the binary divides of male and female, black and white, gay and straight. In contrast to feminist approaches that viewed women as a largely homogeneous group, differentiated only by social class, post-structuralist feminism contests notions of what it means to be female by arguing that there is no such person as a 'typical woman'. Instead, post-structural approaches recognize both the diversity of women's experiences and the multiple factors contributing to gender inequality in society.

Central to post-structuralist analysis is its focus on language and the de-construction of the subject, that is, the multiplicity of individual identities or subject positions. For feminist post-structuralists, this involves revealing how the ways in which we use language reflect historical and cultural narratives or meanings, and how these are gendered. A key concept in post-structural analysis is that of *discourse*.

Much feminist post-structural work draws on the work of Michel Foucault (1979, 1981) and his theories of discourse and the self (see Chapter 10). Foucault argued in *A History of Sexuality* (1981) that 'sex' is not an unequivocal or fixed essence, but is produced, or made intelligible, by complex and historical figurative representations of appropriate and deviant sexuality. That is, what makes for acceptable or 'deviant' sex, and thus regulates individual thought and behaviour, is constructed through nineteenth-century texts, images and ways of talking about sex. These become normalized discourses, or sets of beliefs and understandings reinforced daily in our language practices, and frame the way we understand the world (Weedon, 2004). It is the dominant discourses of femininity (aligned with nature and passivity), which arose in what is known as the Enlightenment Project beginning in the eighteenth century and continued through medico-scientific discourses and practices during the nineteenth and twentieth centuries, that frame and regulate what it means to be a woman. It is these dominant discourses which continue to position women as passive and men as active. Hence the dominant discourses of femininity and leadership undermine women's credence as 'good leaders'.

Once discourses are taken for granted, it is difficult to think, or indeed act, outside this network of meaning. Moreover, for Foucault (1979), discourse is related to power, in that who controls the dominant discourse can determine who has authority and who does not, who is heard and who is not. For Foucault, power is not resident in any individual, male or female, but rather is all-pervasive and evident in what he terms 'regimes of truth' – the dominant types of discourses that are accepted and reinforced through education, media and politics. In the outdoors, it is typically outdoor leaders, managers, directors of outdoor centres and those running outdoor courses – predominantly men – who are the ones 'speaking' about outdoor leadership. They are effectively creating and reinforcing the discourses surrounding qualifications and outdoor leadership, thus determining what is accepted and valued.

Post-structural feminists often draw on the work of Foucault (1981) to explain how dominant forms of masculinity and femininity are constituted historically and culturally, and consequently serve to organize our thought and action. They also draw attention to discourses that intersect with gender, such as those associated with race or class. In doing so, they seek to expose and de-construct binary constructions of gender and highlight the ways in which some (usually male and white) discourses are privileged over others. For example, the history of outdoor education highlights the dominance of military training and physicality in leadership development practices that emerged from the public schools in the UK. Closer analysis reveals the existence of alternative discourses in outdoor education, associated with, for example, personal and social development, environmental awareness and egalitarianism in such movements as the Woodcraft Folk. These discourses would perhaps lead to more women outdoor leaders, as they do not contradict notions of femininity. It is arguable that since these alternative discourses have historically been marginalized and less visible, they have been less popular. Such discourses need to be promoted and made more desirable for students if the hegemonic (dominant) discourses and cultures are to be challenged (Humberstone, 2000).

The availability of alternative discourses enables women to position and re-position themselves at any one time within multiple discourses. For example, a female leader can draw on a particular discourse of education and position herself legitimately within it as outdoor educator or facilitator. An ongoing problem, however, is that while there are multiple discourses, they are often conflicting or contradictory for women. For example, a woman can position herself as a physically strong mountain guide and adventurer, but these discourses conflict with dominant discourses of femininity or of motherhood. As such, women are constantly negotiating their subject positions, with different ones being significant at different times (Allin, 2003). Such conflicting discourses in the outdoors were most noticeable in the case of Alison Hargreaves, who lost her life while descending the summit of K2 and was condemned as an 'unfit' mother for leaving her two children. Donnelly (2004) describes how media attention focused on the loss of a mother to two small children with suggestions that she was 'irresponsible' in her actions. By comparison, media accounts of expectant father and mountain guide Rob Hall lauded his heroism for staying with an incapacitated client on Everest, in the knowledge that he would die if he did not leave the client and descend the mountain.

Theoretically, the focus on language and discourse can make it difficult to analyse the realities of women's lived and embodied experiences in an outdoor profession. Hence some feminist writers have retained attention on the material body, but drawn on post-structuralism to show how women's experiences of their bodies differ due to gendered discourses. Barrett (2005), for example, nicely uses the example of solo portaging a canoe to show how, for a woman, gendered discourses of physicality position her as a 'superwoman', but for a man to portage solo is only what is expected. Dominant gendered discourses, of course, also position men in different ways. For example, for a man on an instructor course, asking for help in decision-making or with carrying his physical load may position him as a weak leader and threaten his masculinity.

For post-structural feminists, then, the focus is on a celebration of differences between women rather than women as a group. In particular, they emphasize the way women are positioned, or position themselves, within multiple identity discourses which are less fixed and more fluid. This approach is consistent with black feminist theory, which stresses the significance of racism and racist discourses (among other factors) in constructing black women's experiences. A potential problem with this perspective, however, is that it risks losing the commonality between women, and thus reduces their power to effect actual change to women's lives.

Conclusion

What we have tried to show in this chapter is that feminism is not a single entity, but rather that there are multiple feminist theories and perspectives. This chapter has dealt with some of the main ones, but it should be recognized that we have only really scratched the surface of feminist theory and research. While feminism has a common interest in understanding women's lives and addressing gender inequality, each feminist theory views the issue of gender and gender inequality in society differently. In applying each to outdoor leadership qualification systems and women's progression within them, it can be seen that each perspective has different explanations and solutions.

Liberal feminism is often seen as 'common sense' and is adopted by men and women uncritically, as it values individualism, minimizes disturbance to the status quo and holds up the ideal of 'the best person for the job'. Radical feminism, on the other hand, is particularly salient in terms of highlighting male power in issues of physicality and in exposing how seemingly innocuous concepts and structures may serve to reinforce male superiority in outdoor qualification systems, while undermining women's 'natural' strengths. Socialist feminists add to the debate through an analysis of patriarchy and capitalism, by explaining how financial and domestic inequalities through women's free labour in the home can disadvantage women's progression through qualification systems. Finally, post-structural feminism has value in uncovering the dominant and emerging discourses of gender, outdoor education and leadership, and in recognizing diversity and providing scope for resistance and challenge.

Each perspective, of course, has its weaknesses. Liberal feminism is perhaps a little naive, radical feminism and socialist feminism over-rely on the often criticized concept of patriarchy, while post-structuralist feminism, with its main focus on language and discourse, negates actual embodied practices and experiences. The beauty of *feminisms*, however, is that they are not static; their theories are constantly being challenged and developed.

So what does this mean for you?

We hope this chapter has caused you to reflect on your beliefs about feminism, feminist theory and its contribution to understanding the gendered dynamics of outdoor leadership. On a practical level, it may lead you to question the extent to which the discourses and practices surrounding outdoor leadership are truly gender neutral. This might involve you reflecting on your personal experiences of the outdoors, and examining the processes involved in qualifying as an outdoor leader. We also hope that knowledge of feminist perspectives will encourage you to challenge taken-for-granted assumptions about masculinity and femininity in your personal professional practice, and strive to take steps towards equality and fairness.

References

Allin, L. (2000) 'Women into outdoor education: Negotiating a male-gendered place', in B. Humberstone (ed.), *Her outdoors: Risk, challenge and adventures in gendered open spaces*, publication no. 66 (pp. 51–68), Brighton: Leisure Studies Association.

Allin, L. (2003) 'Challenging careers for women? Negotiating identities in outdoor education', unpublished PhD thesis, Buckingham University Chilterns College, Brunel University.

Barrett, M.J. (2005) 'Making (some) sense of feminist post-structuralism in environmental education research and practice', *Canadian Journal of Environmental Education*, 10 (Spring), 79–93.

Cherney, I. and London, K. (2006) 'Gender-linked differences in the toys, television shows, computer games, and outdoor activities of 5- to 13-year-old children', *Sex Roles*, 54, 717–26.

Deem, R. (1986) *All work and no play: The sociology of women and leisure*, Milton Keynes: Open University Press.

Donnelly, P. (2004) 'Sport and risk culture', in K. Young (ed.), *Sporting bodies, damaged selves: Sociological studies of sports-related injury* (pp. 29–57), London: Elsevier.

Foucault, M. (1979) *Discipline and punish: The birth of the prison*, Harmondsworth: Penguin.

Foucault, M. (1981) *The history of sexuality: An introduction*, London: Penguin.

Haluza-DeLay, R. and Dyment, J. (2003) 'A toolkit for gender inclusive wilderness leadership', *Journal of Physical Education, Recreation and Dance*, 74(7), 28–32.

Henderson, K. (1996) 'Feminist perspectives on outdoor leadership', in K. Warren (ed.), *Women's voices in experiential education* (pp. 107–17), Dubuque, IA: Kendal/Hunt.

Hornibrook, T., Brinkert, E., Parry, D., Seimens, R., Mitten, D. and Priest, S. (1997) 'The benefits and motivations of all-women outdoor programs', *Journal of Experiential Education*, 20(3), 152–8.

Humberstone, B. (2000) 'The "Outdoor Industry" as social and educational phenomena: Gender and outdoor adventure/education', *Journal of Adventure Education and Outdoor Learning*, 1(1), 21–35.

Loeffler, T.A. (1995) 'Factors that influence women's career development in outdoor leadership', unpublished doctoral dissertation, University of Minnesota, Minneapolis, MN.

McDermott, L. (2004) 'Exploring intersections of physicality and female-only canoeing experiences', *Leisure Studies*, 23(3), 283–301.

Mitten, D. (1992) 'Empowering girls and women in the outdoors', *Journal of Physical Education, Recreation and Dance*, 63(2), 56–60.

ONS (2009) 'Presentation of the gender pay gap', Office for National Statistics position paper.

Online, available at: http://www.ons.gov.uk/ons/rel/social-inequalities/presentation-of-the-gender-pay-gap—ons-position-paper/november-2009/index.html (accessed 29 September 2012).

Rich, A. (1977) *Of woman born: Motherhood as experience and institution*, London: Virago Press.

Royal Yachting Association (2009) 'Equality Action Plan 2009–13'. Online, available at: http://www.rya.org.uk/SiteCollectionDocuments/hr-administration/administration/Equality/Equality%20Action%20Plan%2009-13.pdf (accessed 29 September 2012).

Saunders, N. and Sharp, B. (2002) 'Outdoor leadership: The last male domain?', *European Journal of Physical Education*, 7(2), 85–94.

Sharp, B. (2001) 'Take me to your (male) leader', *Gender and Education*, 13(1), 75–86.

Thompson, S.M. (1999) *Mother's taxi: Sport and women's labor*, Albany, NY: State University of New York Press.

Walby, S. (1990) *Theorising patriarchy*, London: Wiley-Blackwell.

Warren, K. (1996) 'Women's outdoor adventures: Myth and reality', in K. Warren (ed.), *Women's voices in experiential education* (pp. 10–17), Dubuque, IA: Kendal/Hunt.

Warren, K. and Loeffler, T.A. (2006) 'Factors that influence women's technical skill development in outdoor adventure', *Journal of Adventure Education and Outdoor Learning*, 6(2), 107–20.

Weedon, C. (2004) *Identity and culture*, Milton Keynes: Open University Press.

West, A., Green, E., Brackenridge, C.H. and Woodward, D. (2001) 'Leading the way: Women's experiences as sports coaches', *Women in Management Review*, 16(2), 85–92.

Women's Sport and Fitness Foundation (2012) 'Trophy women? National Governing Bodies leadership audit 2011/2012'. Online, available at: http://www.wsff.org.uk/publications/reports/trophy-women-national-governing-bodies-leadership-audit-20112012 (accessed 29 September 2012).

12

IDENTITY POLITICS IN THE OUTDOOR ADVENTURE ENVIRONMENT

Elizabeth C.J. Pike and Johnny Weinstock

> We don't stop playing because we grow old; we grow old because we stop playing.
> *(George Bernard Shaw)*

This chapter will take a critical interactionist approach to understanding the participation and experiences of diverse social groups in outdoor adventure. We will start with an explanation of critical interactionism and move on to examine why adventure has a tradition of being dominated by particular social groups (e.g. young, white, middle-class males). We will then focus on one particular marginalized group – outdoor adventure enthusiasts over the age of retirement – before concluding with some thoughts on ways in which critical interactionism offers insights into how academics and practitioners might transform the outdoor adventure environment by offering opportunities that better meet the needs of participants from a broader range of social groups.

The authors of this chapter have shared backgrounds as trained physical education teachers, whose subsequent careers have adopted a critical approach to the ways in which sporting activities, including outdoor adventure, might contribute to individual development, social life and cultural ideology. One of the authors now works as an academic and the other as a practitioner; we bring these shared and contrasting backgrounds to the writing of this chapter. We will explore how the scholarly world of the academic might illuminate the lived experiences of the practitioner, and examine how the 'real world' scenarios of the practitioner might contribute to a better applied use of social theory by the academic.

Critical interactionism and outdoor adventure

As outlined in Chapter 7, interactionist theory focuses on the social processes through which social worlds are created, and views those worlds through the eyes of the participants themselves. Social worlds are groups of people with shared purposes and values. These social worlds include the interactions that take place between people in outdoor adventure environments – whether in training to become an instructor, as a member of an adventure club, or during casual encounters at a rock face or in the ocean. People give meaning to themselves, others, and the world around them as they interact with other people in these social environments. In so doing, individuals form identities as they integrate their experiences into their sense of who they are and how they are connected with the rest of the world. These identities influence people's decisions and actions, and take into account the consequences of these choices. For example, people may consider: what risk am I taking if I engage in this activity? What benefits are to be gained? What are the possible outcomes for myself, other people in my life and the physical environment? As we evaluate these processes, we become able to develop theories to explain the social organization and dynamics of particular situations.

Interactionist theory has been criticized for failing to consider power relations and the influence of social organizations on people's choices and lifestyles (see Coakley and Pike, 2009). For example, people's ability to become involved in outdoor adventurous activities may be influenced by the school that they attended, the sports clubs that they can afford to join, the facilities that the local government chooses to provide, and social expectations regarding 'appropriate' behaviour (e.g. as a boy/girl, at a certain age). As a result, scholars have combined interactionist theory with critical theory to move beyond merely describing social worlds to a more critical approach of considering how activities can, and should, be organized to better meet the needs of participants (see Coakley and Donnelly, 1999; Beal, 2002). This critical interactionist theory also affords us an understanding of how identities are not fixed; they change as relationships change, as we meet new people and have new experiences – including in the outdoor environment. In this way, people may be agents of change as they consider the choices available to them.

Some of the questions that might be asked by interactionist theorists interested in better understanding outdoor adventure include:

1   What are the characteristics of outdoor adventure cultures, how are they created, and how do they influence people's lives?
2   What are the social processes through which people might become involved with outdoor adventure?
3   How do people give meaning to, and derive meaning from, their outdoor adventure experiences?
4   What happens if people are unable to continue with outdoor adventurous activities?
5   How do people come to define themselves, and be defined by others, as outdoor adventure participants?

(adapted from Coakley and Pike, 2009, p. 52)

We will revisit these questions later in the chapter, after we have examined in more detail the concepts of identity politics and the experiences of one particular social group in the outdoor adventure environment: the older participant.

Identity politics in the outdoor adventure environment

The concept of *identity politics* is used to indicate that some social groups are relatively privileged, while others are oppressed and marginalized. For example, many organized sports and outdoor adventurous activities initially developed during the late 1800s and early 1900s, in countries such as the United Kingdom and the United States of America. The dominant developmental theory at this time emphasized the need for young people to engage in such activities because of their perceived benefits for physical growth and character development (Cook, 2001). However, older people were discouraged from engaging in adventurous activities for fear of overstressing their frail bodies. Similarly, people with disabilities were denied such opportunities in a belief that they may be dangerous and undermine their well-being (Coakley and Pike, 2009). As a result, while outdoor adventurous activities were believed to have physical and mental benefits, older people and disabled people were marginalized and unable to readily access these opportunities.

Furthermore, while some outdoor adventurous activities have challenged participation trends in more traditional sporting activities, it remains the case that most activities are predominantly undertaken by the young, middle-class, white, able-bodied males who also dominate traditional competitive sports (see Wheaton, 2004).

Critical interactionist analyses of identity politics draw on an understanding of such exclusion in order to recommend ways in which individuals and oppressed groups might transform their own sense of self and community through outdoor adventure. In so doing, participants may also develop new opportunities consistent with their identities, values and aspirations. We will now turn our attention to the methods used by critical interactionists to further explore such issues, before giving detailed consideration to one marginalized group – the older outdoor adventurer – as a means of exploring these issues in more detail.

Critical interactionism and research methods

Researchers drawing on critical interactionist ideas generally use ethnographic research methods. This involves researchers immersing themselves in the lives of the social worlds they are studying, so that they might observe the social interactions that create the participants' social worlds and, consequently, their sense of identity. Ethnography, therefore, involves researchers spending extended periods of time with their study participants – observing their behaviour, participating in their daily lives, listening to what is said. In order for this to be critical, and not just descriptive, researchers need to listen to the voices of everyone in these social worlds. This enables them to understand power relations between different groups and to see how people accept or contest these power relations.

This critical approach then allows sociologists to see if there are contradictions between dominant ideals and actual practices, and thus identify areas for promoting social change. For example, if an adventure club claims to be inclusive of all participants but does not actually have equipment that is suitable for people with specific disabilities, a critical interactionist would witness this contradiction, see how participants negotiate and respond to the lived reality, and make recommendations for improved practice. Consider the case of the multi-million-pound award from National Lotto that was given to the elite British public school Eton in return for the use of their facilities for the 2012 Olympic Games. This has been highly criticized as further advantaging the already privileged, with some believing that this cash should have been invested into facilities that would be more accessible to local communities. Critical interactionist research enables such actions and opinions to be questioned, and for recommendations of change to be made to those in positions of power.

We are now going to turn our attention to older people who have experiences of outdoor adventure. The purpose of this next section is to illustrate how listening to the voices of people in particular social worlds can help us to understand their experiences, explore contradictions between ideals and real-world scenarios, and enable us as sociologists to consider the ways in which access to adventurous activities may be more appropriately provided.

The older outdoor adventure enthusiast

Life expectancy is increasing in most countries and, as people live longer, it is likely that there will be increased demand among older people for opportunities to engage in activities with health benefits. Evidence suggests that older people seek social and inclusive activities that emphasize health, fitness and cooperation, rather than those featuring competition and physical force. Take, for example, findings from a study of 'wild swimmers' whose lifestyles contrast with the more usual perception that older people are frail, dependent and socially isolated. One male, aged 64, who wrote about his experiences for the study explained:

> My friends and family take it for granted that I go swimming and know it is a significant part of my life. They are interested and amused at the odd places I have found to swim in when on holiday [e.g. every ocean I've visited from the tropics to the arctic, remote rivers and lakes].
>
> *(see Pike, 2011, p. 499)*

If we adopt a critical interactionist perspective to understanding the lifestyle choices of this swimmer, and others like him, we can see that his comments illustrate the way that identities are fluid and can be changed through interactions with different people and situations. In this way, critical interactionism helps us to make progress in promoting alternative, positive ideas and images of ageing. For example, traditionally there has been an acceptance of what has been termed a 'deficit model' of ageing: that if we can age without disease, this should be regarded as 'healthy ageing'. However, critical interactionism allows us to understand how people derive meaning from outdoor adventure, and create a new sense of self-identity in the process. This has led to a challenge to the deficit model of ageing, with the presentation of a more 'heroic model' of ageing, where older people do not simply have to hope to be free of disease in later life, but can, if they wish, engage in a whole range of activities as they age (Reed *et al.*, 2003).

A relatively recent phenomenon has been the increasing number of 'grown-up gappers': older people who are taking career breaks during which they travel overseas and engage in adventurous activities that are more usually associated with teenagers on a 'gap year'. An industry has now developed to meet the needs of older adventurers, and our critical interactionist perspective helps us to analyse the demand for these programmes. Take, for example, the Travellers Worldwide agency. The company offers volunteer opportunities with numerous examples of the types of outdoor adventurous activities that are offered to participants. Their website states:

> Grown-up Gappers: If you've always thought that gap years and volunteering are for the 18 year olds out there, think again. Whether you're in such a rut and need some time out to refresh your soul and get back your inspiration, or whether you're just travel mad and think it's time for another adventure, we've got the project for you.
>
> *(Travellers Worldwide, 2012)*

The language used on this website demonstrates how these activities can be understood through addressing the questions that we posed at the beginning of this chapter. We'll now answer each of the five questions in turn.

What are the characteristics of outdoor adventure cultures, how are they created, and how do they influence people's lives?

If we return to the key tenets of interactionist theory, we can understand adventure as a cultural phenomenon within which people are encouraged to share values and meanings through interaction with others and the environment, and are able to form and transform identities in so doing. When we adopt a more critical interactionism, we can also explore the institutionalization of outdoor adventure in formal educational curricula, and how this influences people's lifestyles and choices. For example, when discussing Scotland's 'Curriculum for Excellence', Nicol *et al.* (2007) argue that outdoor adventurous activities can encourage young people to become successful learners, responsible citizens, confident individuals and effective participants in societal projects (p. 2). In this way, outdoor adventure is understood as encouraging the development of specific skills and characteristics that are valued in particular societies. Similarly, our wild swimmer and grown-up gappers demonstrate a belief that outdoor adventure can contribute to personal growth and development regardless of the age of the participant. As critical interactionists, we might test these claims and consider whether outdoor adventure always contributes to personal growth, why societies may value characteristics such as confidence, and what is meant by being a responsible citizen.

What are the social processes through which people might become involved with outdoor adventure?

For many, engagement in outdoor adventure has been a consistent feature of their lifestyles. In a conversation with a 70-year-old outdoor educator, we were told that he had always been involved in outdoor adventure and described these activities as 'ageless', since in the outdoors the age of the participant is secondary to the shared pleasure from the activities and environment.

For others who may not have engaged in outdoor activities from an early age, it appears that some may have become involved with outdoor adventure by way of reflecting on their sense of self and having a desire to redefine themselves as a more adventurous type of person; this may have been enabled through participation in activities like wild swimming or the gap-year experience. These decisions to get active can be encouraged by the 'interested' and 'amused' friends and relatives of our wild swimmer, and by companies offering the grown-up gapper experience. These social processes reinforce the acceptability of outdoor adventure in later life.

However, it is important to note that these examples are positive experiences, and there are many older people who are discouraged from participating in such activities, as others have deemed them inappropriate 'at your age' (Laventure, 2007). Our critical interactionist perspective helps us to understand that many people share a belief in the deficit model of ageing, and so will discourage older people from participating in such activities in order to avoid risking damage to a 'frail body'. As critical interactionists, we can challenge such assumptions by presenting the stories that we have heard when listening to the voices of the older participants themselves.

How do people give meaning to, and derive meaning from, their outdoor adventure experiences?

Critical interactionism helps us to understand how older people might engage in outdoor adventure in an effort to subvert the stigma of 'vulnerable' ageing bodies, as these activities and the people with whom they interact may enable them to identify as something other than an 'old person'. In contrast to other sporting activities which take place in 'safer' spaces and which might normally be associated with ageing bodies (Bhatti, 2006), outdoor adventurous activities on mountains, in the air, in the Arctic and in open water may be a sign of the 'agelessness' described by our 70-year-old outdoor educator, who went on to tell us that 'in here [pointing at his head], I'm still 17. Why should age make a difference to what I do?' For others, such activities may even be a conscious display of a youthful risk-taking persona that challenges perceived limitations of the ageing body.

What happens if people are unable to continue with outdoor adventurous activities?

One consequence of increased numbers of older people engaging in such activities has been a recorded increase in the number of accidents and injuries related to outdoor adventure among older people. For example, a report in 2010 indicated that injury claims made by Britons over the age of 70 from sports such as scuba diving, mountaineering and skiing had increased from 5 per cent of total claims in 2006 to nearly 20 per cent in 2010 (Perkins Slade, 2012). This may be partially related to increasing numbers of older people undertaking such activities, as people are living longer, and those with high economic and cultural capital have the resources to engage in them.

However, the high level of reporting of injuries in later life can also contribute to negative stereotypes of older persons and their (in)ability to safely engage in outdoor adventure. For example, some insurance companies attribute these claims to the increasing fragility of the ageing body. Perkins Slade is a large British insurance broker that offers insurance advice and cover for companies including sports organizations. Richard Doubleday, Director of Sport at Perkins Slade, stated: 'While older people may think they are capable of taking risks with their bodies, the reality is that they are more vulnerable' (Perkins Slade, 2012). This provides us with an example of why it is important to adopt a critical interactionist approach that not only explores social worlds through the eyes of the participants, but also looks at the influence of social organizations on people's lifestyles. The message from companies such as Perkins Slade is that older people should carefully consider whether or not they should engage in outdoor adventure; this is a message that is notably different from that given to younger participants. We also know that older people may have to pay higher prices for insurance or may not be able to gain insurance at all, which is in itself a barrier to participation. Our critical interactionist perspective enables us to question such practices, and to consider what may be more appropriate in their place.

How do people come to define themselves, and be defined by others, as outdoor adventure participants?

When we consider the stories of these older participants and combine them with the injury statistics available, our critical interactionist perspective helps us to understand how this may demonstrate what the interactionist theorist Erving Goffman (1967) described as *elements of character*. Goffman argued that the development of character is predicated upon degrees of sacrifice and risk. When a person perceives danger in a situation but proceeds regardless of the risk, this is an indication that they have what Goffman termed *courage*. If, in taking such perceived risks, an individual suffers a setback (whether physical, social or emotional) but continues with the activity with a full display of effort, this is regarded as *gameness*. When older people display courage and gameness, they are able to redefine themselves as other than the vulnerable person proposed by Perkins Slade, and become defined by others as an 'outdoor adventurer'. For example, another swimmer described how, as a 60-year-old woman, her non-swimming friends thought she was 'utterly mad, doing all this exercising', but she continued with the activity regardless.

Engagement in outdoor adventure may also be seen as a means of *impression management*. This is a term that is used to explain how people literally manage their impression of themselves, as a means of getting people to see them differently. Take, for example, the story of another older swimmer who was also a leg amputee:

> I swim with a friend in the sea, it is an activity where my disability is not a disadvantage, and it is always good to keep fit. I tend to train with slightly younger able-bodied people who I can compete with and sometimes beat. While exercising I enjoy the challenge and feel good working hard, I like to keep fit and trim (harder with the years), in my circumstances I cannot afford to put too much weight on. I really enjoy swimming, it is the freedom of not having to wear an uncomfortable restrictive false leg and not being at a disadvantage.
>
> *(male, aged 60); see Pike, 2011, p. 502*

His story illustrates how he is able to fend off the external appearance of an ageing and disabled body and explore what, for him, is his 'true' youthful and fit self beneath the exterior (Goffman, 1963, 1969). The involvement in wild swimming enables him to redefine himself to other people as an outdoor adventure participant, rather than an ageing disabled person.

Future possibilities

By drawing on critical interactionist theory, we are able to see future possibilities for social interaction associated with outdoor adventure, to create environments in which participants have some control over the meaning, purpose and organization of the activities in which they engage. In this way, critical interactionism helps us to understand how we might support the development of outdoor adventurous activities that are relevant to the needs and interests of diverse groups, rather than only to those of the dominant groups.

We started this chapter by recognizing that the majority of outdoor adventurous activities are dominated by young, white, middle-class, able-bodied males. However, it is important to recognize that there is evidence of outdoor adventurous activities enabling participants to renegotiate patterns of gender, racial and class domination that are evident in many traditional sports. For example, women's surfing is among the fastest growing activities, and researchers have argued that pursuits such as skateboarding can transcend barriers of race, gender and class (see Borden, 2001). However, it remains the case that participants in these activities are subject to stereotypes of acceptable gendered and racialized behaviour. Consider, for example, how media coverage of outdoor adventurous activities focuses predominantly on white men, how it excludes women and black or minority ethnic groups (see Kusz, 2004), and how women engaging in these activities are encouraged to do so in a 'feminine' way.

The fastest growing sector of the population is that of older people. In listening to the voices of some older participants in outdoor adventure, we have seen the meanings that are derived from engagement in such activities, and the possibilities they offer for redefining oneself; rather than being defined as vulnerable old people, participants felt energized by their participation and believed that others saw them differently. However, despite these possibilities for agency and self-determination, many institutions and organizations continue to perpetuate the stereotype of the fragility of the ageing body in ways that may be limiting to participants.

We have explored how meanings and values are shared and contested in and through outdoor adventure, and how changes to these may be possible. While these changes are therefore gradual, partial and within existing social structures, critical interactionism offers insights into how marginalized groups might be able to transform their own choices and activities.

Further reading

For an introduction to critical interactionism, try reading chapter 2 of Coakley and Pike (referenced below).

References

Beal, B. (2002) 'Symbolic interactionism and cultural studies: Doing critical ethnography', in J. Maguire and K. Young (eds), *Theory, sport and society* (pp. 353–74), London: Elsevier Science.

Bhatti, M. (2006) '"When I'm in the garden I can create my own paradise": Homes and gardens in later life', *Sociological Review*, 54(2), 318–41.

Borden, I. (2001) *Skateboarding, space and the city: Architecture and the body*, Oxford: Berg.

Coakley, J. and Donnelly, P. (1999) *Inside sports*, London: Routledge.

Coakley, J. and Pike, E. (2009) *Sports in society: Issues and controversies*, London: McGraw-Hill.

Cook, L. (2001) 'Differential social and political influences on girls and boys through education out of doors in the United Kingdom', *Journal of Adventure Education and Outdoor Learning*, 1(2), 43–51.

Goffman, E. (1963) *Stigma: Notes on the management of spoiled identity*, Harmondsworth: Penguin.

Goffman, E. (1967) *Interaction ritual: Essays on face-to-face behavior*, New York: Anchor.

Goffman, E. (1969) *Where the action is*, London: Penguin Press.

Kusz, K. (2004) 'Extreme America: The cultural politics of extreme sports in 1990s America', in B. Wheaton (ed.), *Understanding lifestyle sports: Consumption, identity and difference* (pp. 197–214), London: Routledge.

Laventure, R. (2007) *It's too bloody late for me! Physical activity and older people*, Loughborough: British Heart Foundation National Centre for Physical Activity and Health.

Nicol, R., Higgins, P., Ross, H. and Mannion, G. (2007) *Outdoor education in Scotland: A summary of recent research*, Perth: Scottish National Heritage.

Perkins Slade (2012) *Sport faces huge challenges.* Online, available at: www.perkins-slade. com/news.../for.../sport-faces-huge-challenges (accessed 1 October 2012).

Pike, E. (2011) 'Aquatic antiques: Swimming off this mortal coil?', *International Review for the Sociology of Sport*, 47(4), 492–510.

Reed, J., Cook, G., Childs, S. and Hall, A. (2003) *Getting old is not for cowards*, York: Joseph Rowntree Foundation.

Travellers Worldwide (2012) 'Grown-up gappers'. Online, available at: www.travellersworld wide.com/grown-up-gappers.htm (accessed 1 October 2012).

Wheaton, B. (ed.) (2004) *Understanding lifestyle sports: Consumption, identity and difference*, London: Routledge.

13

GLOBALIZATION, THE MARKET AND OUTDOOR ADVENTURE

Chris Loynes

Access to outdoor adventure in the UK has a long history of power struggles between social classes. In the late nineteenth century the working classes were increasingly able to travel on the cheap railways and were gaining the right to have weekends off and take paid holidays. Some of the middle classes attempted to prevent them reaching places such as the Lake District by opposing the construction of the railways. They claimed that the working classes did not have the education with which to properly appreciate the sublime landscapes of the British coasts and mountains (Williams, 2002). The upper classes had an even more effective strategy, as they owned much of the land and excluded others from it. This led to the mass trespass movements of the 1930s (Glyptis, 1991). It was only in 2000 that the law commonly known as the right to roam restored the right of access for all to open country in England and Wales (Pearlman Hougie and Dickinson, 2000). In Scotland, the 'right to roam' was never lost but was bitterly fought over, nonetheless. Struggles to access land are still not fully resolved, as access to rivers and coastline continues to be a contentious issue (see also Chapter 9).

The colonization and possession of the land by one class to the exclusion of others affected the development of many outdoor activities. In the late twentieth century and early twenty-first century, access to outdoor adventure is again becoming increasingly controlled, but this time, I will argue, it is by aspects of the commercialization of the activities and the locations in which they take place. The impact of these trends on the quality of outdoor experiences and who has access to them is worth understanding, and is thought by some to represent a new struggle as the market attempts its own 'colonization' of the outdoors (Bonnett, 2004). As recently as 2011, protesters challenged the way privatization and charging money for access, in their view, exclude some people from the land and create a barrier to participation in a range of outdoor activities. They also defended the concept of public land and the right to a freedom of access for all.

Despite reassurances from government agencies, the protesters stuck to their arguments and were successful in retaining the public status of the forests. History suggests that they were right to be sceptical. The National Trust, a charity and one of the biggest landowners in the country owning or leasing vast areas in perpetuity on behalf of the nation, has, in the past, also considered charging for access in order to pay for the costs of maintaining the land. The plans were only abandoned because of the impracticality of collecting the fees. However, the question remains as to whether these lands should be understood as national assets managed by the public or charitable sector, and supported from national taxation revenue and charitable giving. Alternatively, should they be funded on the 'user pays' principle, and managed by voluntary and increasingly commercial organizations? This remains a political question about which the public has strong feelings.

Market forces are also at work in a different way within outdoor education. The right to choose the school your children attend and the league tables and reports that help parents to make this choice have created a market in education. Schools are driven to compete on their standards of attainment, which is important but not the sole purpose of education. Outdoor education has been drawn into this trend as professionals and providers are increasingly asked to justify their contribution in relation to how it enhances this attainment.

This chapter will examine the background to commercialization in society. In particular I will use the ideas of commodification, McDonaldization and globalization to consider some of the trends in the outdoor adventure field and their impacts on both recreational and educational forms of outdoor adventure.

The origins of rationalization in outdoor adventure

Outdoor adventure activities emerged at various times during the nineteenth century. A changing attitude to the landscape, encouraged by the Romantic movement and coupled with increasing disposable income and leisure time among wider sectors of society, led to hill-walking, cycling, fishing, and, later, climbing and sailing, becoming popular pastimes.

As explored fully in Chapter 4, Weber (1947) identified the trend in modern societies towards market-led ideas. He defined modernity, the modern way of life in Europe, as a trend towards materialism and rationality (Benton and Craib, 2001). In particular, he was interested in the relationship between the production of material goods and the wider culture. He saw the trends towards *rationalism*, the dominance of means–ends instrumental thought, impacting on many areas of life beyond the commercial world. Weber's critique was aimed especially at the shift from valuing things for themselves to valuing things for the benefits they provide. For example, in outdoor adventure, the value placed on the experience of being outdoors might be replaced by benefits to health, status or education (i.e. the experience is justified in terms of the ends it supports rather than for the intrinsic value of the experience itself). Weber argued that, as modernization progresses, organizations and institutions become more complex and bureaucratic, which leads them to adopt rationalized policies in order to manage the situation. He described this as a means–ends or *instrumental* approach.

The introduction of national governing body awards into recreational sports, including outdoor activities, can be understood as a good example of these rationalizing trends at work. For some people, the training involved in gaining an award may be valued for the performance or coaching skills that are learned. For others, the assessments and awards may be more highly valued for the status or employment opportunities that they offer. In my view, this practice can spiral into a 'paper chase' instead of an effective coach-training strategy, where people engage in training events as preparation for assessments rather than for learning skills.

Weber saw the trend towards rationalization in modernity as increasingly widespread and inevitable. However, another German theorist, Jürgen Habermas (1962), viewed the rationalized world as being in dialogue with the cultural world, so that influence could take place in both directions. Habermas called the rationalized world of commerce and institutions the *system world* and the more creative and organic cultural world the *life world*. Nevertheless, he also thought that the system world was colonizing parts of the life world, such as recreation and education, and that this was a bad trend that reduced quality of life and involvement of the citizen in society.

In earlier articles I have discussed how what Habermas calls the system world is impacting on outdoor adventure recreation and education (Loynes, 1996, 2002). I adopted the term the *algorithmic paradigm* to characterize the impact of the system world on outdoor adventure (Loynes, 2002). The term was coined by Martin Ringer (1999), who saw the same process of rationalization taking place in approaches to group work. To represent the counterpoint of the life world approach, I used a term from the ideas of Robin Hodgkin (1976): *the generative paradigm*. Hodgkin, a professor of education, a mountain guide and a supporter of outdoor education during his time as a head teacher, developed ideas to counter the trends towards rationalization that were already concerning him in the mid-twentieth century. He saw the role of the teacher as one of offering intriguing ideas and experiences to students and then accompanying them in conversation as they made meaning of them and developed them into their identities, their understanding of the world, their values and their sense of direction.

Others, such as Jay Roberts (2011), have noticed the same rationalizing trends in our field. These influences can be encapsulated by thinking about the name we choose to describe the world of outdoor adventure. It is easy to slip into calling it an 'industry', which serves to normalize uncritically what is only a recent colonization of a field that I suggest also makes proud claims to be of the life world, and an antidote to the trends in modernity.

The next section explores some of the concepts that have been developed to aid our understanding of the commercial, rationalized system world. This will help us recognize these processes at work in outdoor adventure education and recreation. I will apply them to some examples in order to provoke further thought and raise questions for you to consider in relation to your own experiences.

Some system world terminology

In understanding the influence of the market on outdoor adventure, it will be helpful to consider some key terms. I will begin by exploring the concept of *commodification*. This is the process in modern economies by which the value of goods or services is not only understood in terms of the intrinsic benefits they provide, but also, or often exclusively, for the extrinsic value (such as money) that can be made from the provision. This is a trend that Weber (1947) predicted, as goods in the market place are increasingly valued for their instrumental worth and not as goods in the wider sense.

I will then look at two related terms. First, I will consider *McDonaldization*, which is a concept that seeks to explain and critique how some commercial activities can be copied from their originating culture and spread around the world, thus colonizing other cultures as they impose one approach on everyone. Second, I discuss *globalization* and why this can be a problem. I will use these terms to discuss some features of outdoor adventure in the modern world and explore why some critics think these trends are a problem.

Commodification

Commodification is easily identifiable in the commercial outdoor adventure world. Bungy jumps and white-water rafting are readily understood as money traps for young people on their gap years and other tourists on holiday. These activities are stripped down to the bare bones of the thrill ride, which is not far removed from a theme park experience. As highlighted in Chapter 2, in bungy jumping, the risks typically managed by the exercise of hard-won skills, knowledge and judgement developed over time – all central to traditional concepts of outdoor adventure experiences – are removed by direct supervision and fail-safe equipment. The same occurs in many commercial raft trips in which a guide manages the oars and the other occupants are merely passengers. While ski resorts leave participants to develop their own skiing abilities on the piste, the designers of the infrastructure of the resort ensure that the place is commodified and very efficient at making money from the skiers, as the chair lifts, food, entertainment and accommodation are all controlled. It is worth the effort of many businesses concerned to create artificial snow when the weather does not play along with the planned ski season window; this in itself is counter to the uncertainty factor that is considered to be a key element of outdoor adventure.

Perhaps commodification is less easily seen in outdoor adventure education than in the recreation examples used above, but Weber (1947) suggests that the instrumentalization of experiences will impact beyond the market place in all walks of life. Habermas recognizes the encroachment of the system world into education and recreation, as they are both realms that he considers to be more properly part of the life world and in which actions are determined by values-oriented thinking rather than instrumentalization (Dodd, 1999).

I think the instrumentalization of outdoor adventure first took place in outdoor centres offering courses in 'adventure training' to corporate clients (Everard, 1993). The first corporate clients were relatively accepting, and believed that well-rounded employees developing in all aspects of their lives would also contribute more to the company. However, at times of financial constraint, managers began to ask for justification for the money spent, in terms of the objective impacts on performance or company profits. Evaluations were administered by training providers and employers began to look for explicit outcomes at the end of the course and impacts back in the workplace. This approach has two limiting aspects to it. First, it narrows the value of the outdoor adventure experience down to that desired by the employer. Second, it reduces the aspirations of the company and the provider to outcomes and impacts that they can quantify, or at least report on, and make claims for. Other, less tangible, 'softer' benefits are often disregarded or reported as 'anecdotal' (Rickinson et al., 2004).

A number of trends in education have led to the same instrumentalist approach being adopted by schools and outdoor adventure providers (Moore, 1987). Schools, also under financial pressure, want to ensure they are getting value for money. Value, in this case, is determined by what will support schools in what is now a competitive market place, where parents choose schools for their children based on nationally published tables ranking schools by their exam results and government inspectors' reports. Schools, and their supporting organizations, now ask for specific outcomes from outdoor adventure programmes. These outcomes are usually linked directly to attainment or indirectly to indicators of the likelihood of better attainment, such as engagement with learning in school, improvements in behaviour and attendance or the development of study skills such as problem-solving or collaborative-working. These are the data that will justify the investment and impact on league tables and student uptake.

Of course, outdoor adventure can provide some or all of these outcomes and these are good things. The point that critics of these trends make is that, as for corporate training, the focus of what is worth doing is narrowed down to the desired and measurable outcomes. Naturally, teachers can still value the other 'intangible' benefits of personal, social and environmental education. In my view, some even resist the trend by refusing to engage with the encroachment of the system world when they are away on residential courses, and focus on appreciating the life world – the 'breath of fresh air' – as much as the children. The issue here is that the outdoor experience has become a means to an end, and this end has been narrowed to outcomes linked with academic progress and employability, rather than with the wider educational benefits for which outdoor adventure education has been historically valued.

Commodification is the initial step towards two other issues first described as being at work in the world of commerce: *McDonaldization* and *globalization*. Both of these ideas can help us more deeply understand trends in the world of outdoor adventure.

McDonaldization and globalization

Ritzer (1993) identified how a successful commercial model could be 'scaled up' by branding a product that was of a predictable quality wherever you bought it. He used McDonald's restaurants to show how the burger became an international dish that not only looks and tastes the same throughout the world, but which is provided from lookalike shops where even the transaction with the customer is scripted to ensure efficiency and predictability. This approach gave the company control over the market, and allowed McDonald's to become a global corporation. This is a good example of the process of globalization, and the international trends that increasingly bring about the integration of markets, ideas and world-views. You will be able to think of many examples of globalization of this kind.

It is helpful to consider that globalization, which in this context is being critiqued, need not always be understood as a bad thing; globalization is not being demonized as such. Many cultural aspects, such as sport and the arts, can be thought of as having positive impacts on our understanding of ourselves as a diverse species with one world to share.

Ritzer (1993) thought that the problem with McDonaldization was that it uses the rational approach of the market to create an efficient brand that can be imposed throughout the world. For example, McDonald's, he claims, devalues local cultural fast food practices and traditions that hold a richer meaning as a part of the indigenous and commercial life of each place. The marketing power of international companies is able to encourage consumers to emphasize certain values, such as our taste for cheap, fatty and salty foods, over the values we attach to healthier foods that are produced in season by local workers being paid fair wages, and which have higher ethical standards of environmental impact and animal welfare. Much is lost for the commercial gain of a corporation not even located in the country affected. That is not to say that local always means better or more ethical. It is to suggest that local production, in context with the culture and environment of the place, contributes more to the expression of culture in that place and can be more readily influenced to produce to higher standards. It is the possibility of a process by which local people can be engaged in these important aspects of food production, rather than be excluded from them, that is at stake.

Ritzer (1993) extended his critique of the fast food industry by suggesting that society is taking on the same characteristics. For example, McDonaldization can be applied to outdoor adventure experiences. They, like the food industry, can be a rich combination of elements embedded in a local culture, history and environment. They can be embedded in a culture's history, for example our mountaineering and polar exploration exploits celebrated throughout British culture and not just by mountaineers. And they can have potentially rich forms of current expression. Consider the way in which health and well-being are currently being promoted valuing fitness and contact with nature in the British countryside. This is leading to changes in policy and funding that encourage participation in outdoor adventure activities. As a consequence, more doctors are now prescribing a good walk as part of a recognized treatment for a range of medical conditions, and therapists are increasingly going for a walk with clients rather than having them lie on a couch (Natural England, 2009). Outdoor adventure is also a social event, both in relation to the people you are active with and the sub-culture that arises around the activity. These activities also take people out into certain landscapes and environments that can form the central motivation for taking part. In this case, the activity as a means to an end (as opposed to the experience of which the activity is one part) can be thought of positively, as it provides a way for people to visit remote or beautiful places and see unusual wildlife and scenery.

The McDonaldization of outdoor adventure

A good example of McDonaldization from the field of outdoor adventure is the challenge course (also known as high ropes course – see also Chapter 10). In the article 'Adventure in a bun' (Loynes, 1996), I highlighted the McDonaldization of adventure by comparing it to the mass production of hamburgers. Roberts (2011) also refers to challenge courses and activities in his recent critique of market-driven forms of outdoor adventure in education. Popularized in the USA through widespread practice in both youth and corporate training markets, the challenge course and the 'processing' techniques used to reflect on the experience were celebrated in a number of textbooks that were then used as templates for the construction and facilitation of such courses around the world. When I witnessed the construction of possibly the first one to be built in India, the director of the training organization enthused to me about the new resource because it meant that he could 'provide the same training to the executive of a multinational client here in India that they would receive in the USA or Europe'. The efficiency and consistency resulting from the McDonaldization of outdoor adventure training was being explicitly encouraged by the clients.

As Roberts (2011) points out, it is not that challenge courses are offering necessarily bad experiences. They have a contribution to make. However, they lend themselves to a universal approach and to McDonaldization in a field that has previously valued diversity brought about by the environmental and cultural contexts in which they are practised.

It is not easy to McDonaldize a relationship with the environment or a group, but it is possible to disembed the activity and locate it elsewhere. The recent history of climbing moving from crags to indoor climbing walls is an example of the experience called climbing being radically altered by disembedding the activity from the context in which it was originally located. This process of transferring an activity from one context to another creates the potential for rich new experiences to emerge. It also creates the possibility of McDonaldization rationalizing the experience down to a small number of key elements that can be branded and marketed globally.

When an activity is McDonaldized, it is no longer part of a cultural story, and nor does it explore a particular landscape. It becomes a replicable structure, often with the same elements everywhere. While it remains a social activity, one of the 'strengths' of this approach, especially in education, is that individual elements of the challenge course can be constructed to determine the character and process of social engagement. This engagement can promote, for example, specific ways of team building that are underpinned by the latest popular abstract psychological theory (the globalization and McDonaldization of theories as an aspect of outdoor adventure education and training is another dimension to this issue), rather than a group working organically in the context of their culture, where participants determine roles and tasks, work out what the experience means to them, and how best to get things done.

Even in basic team-building programmes, teachers are already reporting students who, having done barrels and planks yet again ('we did this in year four, Miss!'), roll out the expected remarks about trust, teamwork and communication; they know what to say rather than say what they know. This hardly warrants the term 'adventure', as the anticipated depth of experience in the activity has evaporated. The activity has become a routine that is disconnected from all the rich experiences of self, others and the environment that outdoor adventure education claims to value.

McDonaldization is one expression of the wider phenomenon of globalization that features the spread of ideas, culture and institutions, as well as businesses, around the world. Within globalization is the potential to celebrate the diversity of life worlds from many different cultures. There is also the possibility of imposing the system world of one dominant power source across the globe. This struggle for the colonization of the world is taking place within all walks of life, and outdoor adventure is not immune.

Andy Brookes (2002b), an Australian academic of outdoor adventure, illustrates the issues associated with globalization in his writing about the colonization of Australia by UK and USA outdoor practices. He says that not only did the early colonists attempt to turn the strange Australian landscape into one that looked familiar, but also that when outdoor adventure entered the culture in both education and recreation, participants and leaders alike travelled hundreds of miles in order to participate in outdoor activities such as climbing and kayaking that were popular in the UK and the USA. He argues that this occurred despite a lively emerging Australian tradition of outdoor living and without thought for what outdoor activities might have been undertaken locally that were environmentally and culturally appropriate (Brookes, 2002a, 2002b; Payne, 2002). The formalization of climbing and kayaking, he argues, has created the potential for them to become McDonaldized. This may be unintentional, but it is exactly what Weber (1947) was concerned about when he described the pervasive influence of the market on wider culture. Surfing, skiing, diving and other outdoor adventure activities have all been critiqued for this globalized imposition of an activity on a place and a culture; see Pedersen (2003) for a Norwegian case study and Payne (2002) for an Australian kayaking equivalent.

As different kinds of space/time borders are crossed, it is possible to critique climbing walls and snow domes that provide indoor 'outdoor' activities as 'colonizers' of urban settings. Likewise, high ropes courses built on poles instead of in trees have enabled these structures to offer their experiences in un-wooded places. These trends can also be understood as strategies that offer businesses certain ways of competing in market places otherwise closed to them. At the same time, the migration from settings that rely on natural features with local and seasonal variability to constructed settings reflects the rationalization of the activity on a global scale. This trend has led to the emergence of international businesses building and managing large-scale, McDonaldized 'outdoor' facilities.

It is not only businesses that can be accused of McDonaldization. Government policies can also act in similar ways. For example, UK Sport frequently attaches targets for participation by minority ethnic groups to grants given to sporting bodies (Cronin and Mayall, 1998). National Parks also set similar targets linked to funding. It can be argued that this is a good thing, as it encourages more opportunities for marginalized groups to access these wild places. This kind of policy trend can also be viewed as one dominant culture imposing its cultural sporting preferences over another (Pedersen, 2003) and thereby creating new market opportunities in the process. Only careful consultation with the groups concerned can reasonably distinguish which is which.

Is it always a bad thing?

The criticisms of the trends in commodification, McDonaldization and globalization can be thought of as implying a wider criticism of commercialization. While this may also be open to criticism, it has been shown to offer benefits in the power relations within a sport. Edwards and Corte (2010) write about the commercialization of BMX biking in one American resort. They highlight that it matters who has control of the commercial activity and how this power is exercised. They noticed in their study that the commercial aspects of the sport were largely controlled by members of the BMX community and that they would often use their power to develop better locations and equipment, provide information, encourage access to and the promotion of the sport and other 'goods' for the BMX culture. In this situation, the sport has been partly commercialized but not commodified. Edwards and Corte point out that, because the market is a small and specialist one, it is not of interest to bigger businesses and so escapes the risk of commodification. They noted that corporate interests restrain their impact on the sport to the peripheries, and market elsewhere the food, drinks, accommodation and 'off-piste' clothing that is already scaled up and 'McDonaldized'. While there are still potential issues with small-scale commercial activity, for example the problems connected with the cost of participation brought about by the cost of what is regarded as appropriate equipment, these are not straightforward and have to be balanced against the potential benefits that come with a degree of commercialization.

Restoring the conversation between the system and the life world out of doors

Outdoor adventure has a rich and varied philosophical base. A main strand of this argues that the outdoors is a space in which it is possible to escape from the constraints of the everyday world and feel a sense of freedom, to restore the wildness in a person's spirit. This foundation is strongly allied to Habermas's idea of the life world (Dodd, 1999). Seen this way, the outdoors can be thought of as a space in which the ideas and values of the life world can be heard and developed. Restored and rehearsed, the values can accompany the participant back into the everyday world and contest the encroachment of constraining factors, such as those of globalization and Habermas's system world. This is a struggle. Some people can treat outdoor adventure as escape – a therapeutic restoration, a place where it is possible to feel a sense of well-being, if only temporarily. Others find it hard to return to the system world and so become almost full-time adventurers, who are unable to accept the limits of an increasingly constrained modern way of life. If Habermas is right in saying that it is possible for the system world and the life world to be in dialogue, and for the life world to influence the direction of the system world, then spaces such as those created by outdoor adventure become important cultural phenomena. From this perspective, it matters a lot if the system world of McDonaldization and the worst aspects of commercialization and globalization colonize the world of outdoor adventure.

With this in mind, the language used in outdoor adventure circles is important. It can support the dialogue between outdoor adventure as the life world and outdoor adventure as the system world, or it can privilege, sometimes unintentionally, the colonization of this aspect of our culture by the system world. Roberts (2011) proposes that we reinstate the term 'outdoor field' instead of 'outdoor industry', as it more accurately reflects the wider forms of practice that have become marginalized by the word 'industry' as an umbrella term. 'Field', Roberts thinks, implies a mix of practices, in no particular hierarchy, which share some common themes while valuing a diversity of forms. He argues that this would be a much more equitable and creative place. I have argued that we should be careful when we use metaphors from the industrial world (e.g. framing, processing, funnelling, front-loading) to describe the processes of outdoor adventure education (Loynes, 2002). These terms are taken from the language of the production line and the computer.

Concluding thoughts

I have focused on the ways in which outdoor adventure crosses national boundaries. Globalization and McDonaldization are not limited to geography. What do you think about the construction of artificial facilities replicating rural outdoor adventure in urban areas – climbing walls, white-water rapids and ski slopes, for example? Would it be more appropriate to develop forms of outdoor adventure that emerge from this environment? BMX bikes and skateboards might be examples. Or do you think that equity for ethnic groups should be judged on their participation in the outdoor adventure activities that are popular with the dominant ethnic group – higher rates of participation by Asian ethnic groups, for example? Perhaps there are cultural factors that could lead to different forms of practice or even just the same activities but understood in a different way. If you consider these as examples of colonization, how would this affect your understanding and your actions?

Anthropologists point out that most of our cultural practices originate from other cultures. The key point is not that we pick up new ideas from other people and places. It is that the power relations involved need to be considered, as these new forms of practice are taken from one culture and then impact on the new culture and environment into which they are introduced.

Further reading

If you want to deepen your thinking on this issue, it is worth reading the two articles I wrote for more background to the ideas in this chapter (Loynes, 1996, 2002). Brookes's (2002a) article is one of several he has written on the colonization of Australian outdoor practices by northern hemisphere outdoor life. Of course reading Ritzer's book (1993) will give you a much better idea of the central critique offered here, and Roberts's book (2011), especially the chapter on the market, will give you more insight into this phenomenon at work in outdoor adventure. For a theoretical take on how to counter these trends within education, you could do no better than to read *Born Curious* by Robin Hodgkin (1976). All titles are referenced below.

References

Benton, T. and Craib, I. (2001) *Philosophy of social science*, Basingstoke: Palgrave.

Bonnett, M. (2004) *Retrieving nature: Education for a post-humanist age*, London: Routledge.

Brookes, A. (2002a) 'Gilbert White never came this far south: Naturalist knowledge and the limits of universalist environmental education', *Canadian Journal of Environmental Education*, 7(2), 73–87.

Brookes, A. (2002b) 'Lost in the Australian bush: Outdoor education as curriculum', *Journal of Curriculum Studies*, 34(4), 405–25.

Cronin, M. and Mayall, D. (1998) *Sporting nationalisms: Identity, ethnicity, immigration and assimilation*, London: Routledge.

Dodd, N. (1999) *Social theory and modernity*, Malden, MA: Polity Press.

Edwards, B. and Corte, U. (2010) 'Commercialization and lifestyle sport: Lessons from 20 years of freestyle BMX in "Pro-Town, USA"', *Sport in Society*, 13(7/8), 1135–51.

Everard, B. (1993) *The history of development training* [Monograph, self-published].

Glyptis, S. (1991) *Countryside recreation*, Oxford: Longman.

Habermas, J. (1962) *The structural transformation of the public sphere: An inquiry into a category of bourgeois society*, Cambridge: Polity Press.

Hodgkin, R. (1976) *Born curious: New perspectives in educational theory*, London: Wiley.

Loynes, C. (1996) 'Adventure in a bun', *Journal of Adventure Education and Outdoor Leadership*, 13(2), 52–7.

Loynes, C. (2002) 'The generative paradigm', *Journal of Adventure Education and Outdoor Learning*, 2(2), 113–26.

Moore, R. (1987) 'Education and the ideology of production', *British Journal of Sociology of Education*, 8(2), 227–42.

Natural England (2009) 'Our natural health service: The role of the natural environment in maintaining healthy lives'. Online, available at: http://publications.naturalengland.org.uk/publication/31045 (accessed 28 September 2012).

Payne, P. (2002) 'On the construction, deconstruction and reconstruction of experience in "critical" outdoor education', *Australian Journal of Outdoor Education*, 6(2), 4–21.

Pearlman Hougie, D.J. and Dickinson, J.E. (2000) 'The right to roam: What's in a name? Policy development and terminology issues in England and Wales, UK', *European Environment*, 10(5), 230–8.

Pedersen, K. (2003) *Nature and identity: Essays on the culture of nature*, Bergen, Norway: Senter for kulturstudier.

Rickinson, M., Dillon, J., Teamey, K., Morris, M., Choi, M.Y., Sanders, D. and Benefield, P. (2004) *A review of research on outdoor learning*, Preston Montford, UK: Field Studies Council.

Ringer, M. (1999) 'The facile-itation of facilitation? Searching for competencies in group work leadership', *Scisco Conscientia*, 2, 1–19.

Ritzer, G. (1993) *The McDonaldization of society*, New York: Sage.

Roberts, J. (2011) *Beyond learning by doing*, New York: Routledge.

Weber, M. (1947) *The theory of economic and social organisation*, New York: Oxford University Press.

Williams, J. (2002) *Wordsworth: Critical issues*, Basingstoke: Palgrave.

14

OUTDOOR ADVENTURE IN A CARBON-LIGHT ERA

Kate Rawles

> You do not need to fly to the other side of the planet to do an expedition. You do
> not need to be an elite athlete, expertly trained, or rich to have an adventure.
>
> *(Alastair Humphreys)*

This chapter examines outdoor adventure from the perspective of climate change
and the need to tackle it. I'll argue that climate change raises some really difficult
questions for all modern societies in which adventure is valued, and for any of us
who are citizens of these societies. This is especially so in relation to adventures that
involve long-distance flying. The good news is that there are many opportunities
to reduce carbon footprints while still adventuring, and many 'win-wins' – although
leadership and guidance are urgently needed in this area. Perhaps even more importantly, I'll argue that adventures have, potentially, an extremely positive role to play
in contemporary society. Adventures can give us opportunities to question and
change some of the most problematic features of our 'normal' Western lives. In
exploring these issues, I will not focus on any one author or set of concepts, as has
been the case with the previous chapters in this book. Instead, at appropriate points
in the chapter, I will identify the relevance of the theories that have been discussed
by authors of other chapters, and indicate where else in this book you can find more
information on each of these.

Adventure and climate change

Mike Berners-Lee, in his hugely helpful book *How Bad Are Bananas: The Carbon
Footprint of Everything*, tells the story of a friend with a carbon dilemma (2010).
Should he dry his hands on paper towels or use a hot-air hand-drier? Having duly
done the calculations, the result came out slightly in favour of Dyson air-blades over
paper towels, with conventional hot-air driers coming in third. The real point,

though, was that the friend was a frequent transatlantic flier. From a carbon-emissions perspective, flying is *tens of thousands* times more impactful than hand-drying of any kind (see, for example, Monbiot, 2006, Chapter 9; Berners-Lee, 2010, p. xii). Berners-Lee argues that we need to develop a more informed and more effective 'carbon instinct' (p. xi), and hone our ability to focus on the things that will actually make a significant difference and not sweat the small stuff.

The big stuff, in the adventure context, is obvious: travel – especially flying. The average carbon footprint of a UK citizen is somewhere in the region of nine tonnes per year. This is typical for much of Europe. In the USA it is about eighteen (see, for example, the World Bank Group, 2012). In order to achieve 'safe' levels of climate change, in an equitable way, this needs to reduce to between one and two tonnes per person per year (Monbiot, 2006, p. 173). A single transatlantic flight is a little over one tonne. That's almost an entire year's carbon budget in one go! This is also an example of the ways in which we are interdependent with the activities of people and institutions globally (see Chapters 9 and 13).

From an adventure exploration perspective, this is clearly very challenging. Suppose, like me, you value travelling to far-away lands and you find overseas adventures especially gratifying. They may be so important to you that they form part of your individual habitus (see Chapter 8). Yet, having read up on the issue, you agree that long-distance flying and other energy- and carbon-intensive adventures have a very high environmental price – so high it is contributing to changes that are putting our own future, and that of millions of other species, at risk. Can the benefits of adventure possibly justify such extraordinary costs? Whatever the answer, flying is considered utterly normal across industrialized and industrializing societies. We take for granted our freedom to fly and we feel entitled to do so. Why should we stop? We're just doing what's normal. But then suppose you realize, reluctantly, that the fact that something is 'normal' makes it neither right nor wise. And frequent flying, unfortunately, can no longer be understood as either. It seems we not only need to find ways of reducing carbon footprints in relation to adventure, but that we need *to rethink what is normal* more generally. Given the relatively short timescale we have to tackle climate change (see p. 152 below), it is clear we need leadership, not followership, in this area, and we need it fast.

How, then, as someone who values adventure, do you respond? How *should* we respond to this dilemma? What would it mean to show climate leadership in this context? Can we keep what we value about adventures while reducing their carbon footprint? Can we harness the power of adventures to help rethink some of the more problematic aspects of 'normal' modern life? Or should we just ignore the challenge of climate change and carry on as usual?

What is adventure?

Before trying to answer these questions, it is probably worth taking a step back and considering what counts as having an adventure of any kind. My own conception of adventure was heavily influenced by a slightly odd mixture of books by Wilfred

Thesiger and the Crane cousins. The more I read of Thesiger, striding across the world's deserts, marshes and mountains with local guides, a handful of rice and a water container, and the Cranes, cycling up Kilimanjaro before mountain bikes were even invented or running the length of the Himalayas in training shoes, with one spare sock and a sawn-off toothbrush between them (and overtaking fully kitted-out, military-style expeditions on the way), the less I felt that I could become an adventurer myself – much as I dreamt of doing so.

For these 'expedition' adventurers, an adventure was clearly something you did in a remote/faraway/novel/wild place – ideally with some sort of 'different' people or societies thrown in for good measure. On top of that, adventures involved challenging feats of physical, and often mental, endurance. There was always a real chance that the adventurer wouldn't quite make it, forced back by conditions that were too hard, high, long or hot. Ideally, the venture would be built around a journey or an exploit that no-one had ever done before. It would have just the right amount of risk – neither so much that the expedition was doomed from the outset, nor so little that success was a foregone conclusion. And the whole thing would be tackled with a stiff upper lip, minimal kit and unfailing humour in adversity.

If Thesiger's adventures are taken as archetypal, it may well seem that long-distance travel and adventure are inevitably entwined. Reading Thesiger and the Cranes as a teenager, though, the main thing that struck me about adventures was not their high carbon footprint, but that they always seemed out of reach. Adventurers were not ordinary. They were other beings. It would be unbelievably arrogant to even dream of aspiring to them, especially for someone like me – rubbish at school sports, on the weedy side and, what's more, a girl (see Chapter 11 for a more detailed analysis of gender roles and feminist theories, and Chapter 12 for a critical interactionist discussion of identity politics more broadly). It took a while before I realized that adventure is a relative concept and that cycling out of the various Scottish towns I lived in and into the hills was as good a place as any to start. Over the years I got bolder and cycled across Scotland (east to west) and then to France, where I followed the Rhone River from its mouth to the source in the Swiss Alps. I had no idea I could cycle that far. I could, and I loved it. I loved the way cycling brings taken-for-granted landscapes back into glorious focus; the way people come and chat if you arrive by bike; the way you are really *in* the environment you're cycling through – smelling and hearing and feeling it. I loved the physical challenge and the wonderful feeling of getting stronger, fitter and leaner as the trip progressed. Cycling in mountains – hot sunny ones for preference – became my thing. And suddenly, there I was, an ordinary person, having adventures.

Years (and many long miles) later I would argue that this is an important characteristic of adventures, especially when they are loosened from the Thesiger mould and defined a bit more widely; 'ordinary' people can have them. Many other writers and commentators confirm this. A young man who left his Yorkshire house on a bike and kept going – now known as round-the-world-cyclist Alastair

Humphreys – suggests that: 'Adventure is stretching yourself; mentally, physically or culturally. It is about doing what you do not normally do, pushing yourself hard and doing it to the best of your ability' (Humphreys, 2012, para 3). Miles and Priest (1990, p. 1), in their classic book *Adventure Education*, suggest that: 'To adventure is to venture forth into the unknown, to undertake an activity that has an uncertain outcome for the adventurer and may be risky or dangerous.'

If these are taken as the central characteristics of adventure – some form of personal challenge or stretch, plus genuine uncertainty about the outcome – then Thesiger's exploits would certainly qualify of course, as would those of other 'classic' adventurers like Scott and Shackleton, for example. So, too, would escapades involving cycling – or sea-kayaking or hill-walking or the other unusual, exciting or daring activities discussed in this book. These activities can offer physical and mental challenge. They can offer the chance to revel in that fantastic feeling of being truly awake and truly there, on the rock or the wave or the snow – alive in that moment and nowhere else. They can offer the opportunity to explore somewhere or something new (at least new to you) or to explore a relatively familiar place in a new way, and perhaps reawaken curiosity about the people and creatures you encounter in the process. These adventures can offer the satisfaction gained from pushing yourself that bit further towards achieving something you really weren't sure you could. Understanding adventure in this way, and pursuing it through activities like these, open up the potential for adventure that is widely accessible. As Humphreys (2012) says, you do not need to be rich or super-fit to do these things. There *are* barriers to engagement with adventure, of course, and some of these are considered in other chapters. Nevertheless, a huge number of people can, and do, bring adventure into their lives if they really want to.

This perspective also suggests that adventures can, at least sometimes, be had closer to home without losing what is centrally of value about them. This in turn points to one way in which adventure and carbon-light living could become considerably more compatible. We'll return to this shortly. First, though, why is there a focus on climate change anyway?

Climate change: all is not well in the 'outdoors'

Many of us will have experienced the sense of being a small and insignificant speck in the wider scheme of things. It might happen while adventuring in a mountain range, or in response to the immense power of the ocean. The feeling that accompanies this shift in perspective is often oddly positive – even liberating. If we are smaller than minute, then our worries and preoccupations can scarcely register.

However, while we may feel tiny as individuals, our combined impact on the 'outdoors' in which most adventures take place is, in fact, immense. Adventurers are often well-schooled in the art of camp-craft, litter-picking and other ways in which our negative environmental impacts can be kept to a minimum at a local level. By contrast, at the global level we have so fundamentally altered the world's ecological and climactic systems – the systems of which we are a part and on which we depend

– that geologists are debating whether the current geological era should be named the *Anthropozene*: the human era. It is not meant as a compliment. As a species, our impacts on other species and systems are now on a scale hitherto achieved only by the shift of tectonic plates or the emergence of photosynthesizing life. Climate change is perhaps the best-known aspect of this current era, and among the most significant in terms of its potential – and actual – consequences for life on the planet.

In the morass of information about climate change, it is helpful to extract five key points. First, there is good news as well as bad news. The good news is twofold: there is almost certainly still time to tackle climate change – as long as we act effectively and fast – and there are many 'win-wins' to be had in the process.

Second, we need to be really clear about what we know and what is still uncertain, and the certainties include the fact that it's happening. For all the debate in the media and elsewhere, there is a truly astounding degree of consensus across the international scientific community in terms of what might be called the 'big picture': a) global climate change is under way; b) human activities are contributing to it; and c) it is potentially very bad news. A great deal of uncertainty exists in relation to local and regional questions, in terms of what exactly global climate change will mean in particular places at particular times. That it is well under way is (unfortunately!) not in doubt.

Third, concern about this issue is not on a par with other personal interests and passions (e.g. I'm into climate change, you're into skiing or chess) and nor, really, is it similar to other 'good causes' and campaigns. If we don't deal with it, our future as a species is in the balance. Tackling climate change – and other global-level ecological problems – underpins the possibility of pursuing all other interests, passions, campaigns and causes.

Fourth, the main human contribution to climate change is our escalating use of fossil fuels and the destruction of forests. There are discussions of the processes of industrial development from the perspective of various social theories in Chapters 2, 3, 9 and 13 in particular. In this chapter, I wish to extend these debates to consider another consequence of economic and manufacturing 'progress'. In essence, the industrial revolution has been powered on ancient sunlight. We have taken carbon, formed from long-dead plants and stored for millions of years under the surface of the earth in the form of oil, coal and gas, and burned it. This has given us a vast new source of energy and the many, undeniable, life-transforming benefits of industrialization. It has also released immense amounts of carbon dioxide into the atmosphere, where it and other 'greenhouse gases' trap heat from the sun. At the same time, we have destroyed millions of acres of forest that would otherwise act as a carbon sink; this adds up to an appalling double-whammy. The result is an increase in the natural 'greenhouse effect' and an overall rise in the average temperature of our planet. How much bigger an increase we can expect depends on what we do next. The Intergovernmental Panel on Climate Change (IPCC, 2007) predicts rises in the earth's average temperature of between 1.6 and 6.4 degrees Celsius by the end of the century. Most 'business as usual' scenarios show us hurtling towards a three or four degree rise.

The fifth point is that we need to get real – about both the scale of the challenge this presents us with and the consequences of not rising to it. Four degrees colder (the difference between the average global temperature now and at the time of the last ice age) and we're covered in ice a mile thick. Four degrees *hotter* changes the climate beyond recognition. The implications of a three or four degree rise for our ability to meet our basic needs – to provide food, water and security – are dire. The implications for other species are worse. The biologist E.O. Wilson argues that, given the degree of current climate change, on top of other impacts, we are likely to lose 50 per cent of all our wild species by the end of the century (see, for example, Whitty, 2007). In sum, runaway climate change is not just a bit of bad weather. It will bring us radical, sudden and irreversible change, which will cause social and ecological chaos. As authors have argued elsewhere in this book (see Chapters 9 and 13), human lives are globally interdependent.

To keep climate change at relatively safe levels, and to avoid 'runaway' or dangerous levels, most analysts agree that we need to stabilize at a rise of no more than two degrees. To do this, our emissions of carbon dioxide (as well as our impacts on forests and other natural carbon off-setting ecosystems) need to fall dramatically. Most analysts argue that CO_2 and other greenhouse gas emissions need to reduce by 80 per cent by 2050 across the industrialized world. *Eighty per cent.* Some argue for 90 per cent (Monbiot, 2006). A considerable chunk of these reductions needs to happen within the next decade.

Responses

Let's suppose for the moment that you accept this. You agree that the basic climate change science is extremely hard to refute and that the consequences of not tackling the issue are truly appalling. To return to the questions introduced earlier, how, as someone who values adventure, do you respond? How *should* we respond to this dilemma? What would it mean to show climate leadership in this context?

One possible approach is essentially a form of cost–benefit analysis. Attempting to balance or justify costs in relation to benefits is a strategy used in a wide range of contexts. It is one way of thinking about adventure and climate change, too. The approach can be broken down into stages.

First, given that some sort of cost in terms of carbon footprint is almost always entailed by adventure, it is reasonable to suggest we should think critically about aims. Arguably, a great deal of 'mainstream' adventure in industrialized societies such as the UK, the USA, Japan or Australia continues in a long tradition of personal challenge: climb the three highest mountains in the UK in twenty-four hours, climb the seven highest summits in the world, row across the Atlantic Ocean, run a marathon on every continent, climb Everest. Some, but not all, of these have become increasingly commercialized (for discussions of the commodification of adventure see Chapters 4 and 13). Many involve genuinely astonishing feats of endurance and tenacity. Typically – though not always – they are about individual achievement rather than, for example, national glory or conquest (for discussions of this from a range of theoretical perspectives see Chapters 3, 5, 7, 8 and 12). A relatively new dimension of adventures are the expeditions that, in addition to offering the context for personal challenge and development, are organized as fund-raisers or awareness-raisers for a diverse range of causes. And, of course, there are the gap-year overseas expeditions that often aim to contribute something worthwhile to the local community and/or conduct useful scientific research, while trying to promote the personal development and growth of those involved (see, for example, Pike and Beames, 2007).

As individuals embarking on adventure we can ask what we personally hope to achieve, and whether these aims are worthwhile. Could they be strengthened? Given the climate context, is it really a laudable aim to bungy jump on all five continents? If the answer to this seems straightforwardly negative, how about climbing the highest peak on all five continents or other aims purely focused on personal challenge? Where do you draw the line? Could challenge-focused aims be linked with personal development or perhaps a wider social goal? And if so, does this strengthen them? What criteria would you recommend for identifying aims as worthwhile? Once you've established the best possible overall aims for a given adventure, the rest of the process is essentially about reducing the carbon costs as far as possible, on the one hand, and increasing the benefits as far as possible on the other.

Stages two to five focus on suggestions for reducing carbon costs. Stage two is to ask whether your adventure aims could be achieved without long-haul travel. Alastair Humphreys (2012, para 1) has worked on inspiring exactly this approach and wrote that, for him, '2011 is the year of the microadventure: a whole year when, instead of exotic foreign adventures, I am committed to trying to encourage people to get outside, get out of their comfort zone, go somewhere they've never been, go on a microadventure. An adventure that is close to home, cheap, simple, short, and yet very effective.' Close-to-home adventures don't have to be short, of course. And they don't have to be easy. Anyone who has read (or emulated!) Bryan Wilson's epic *Blazing Paddles* (2008) – his account of sea-kayaking around Scotland – will know that closer-to-home expeditions can be every bit as daunting as those undertaken further afield (see also Chapters 7 and 12 for interactionist critiques of this phenomenon).

The third stage involves questioning your mode of travel more generally. If there *is* something irredeemably important about the location of your adventure 'abroad', or even if your destination is relatively close by, is it possible to get there in a carbon-light way? Travelling across France to the Pyrenees by train has a much lower footprint than flying there, and a minibus load of people doing the same journey has a lower footprint than either. Cycling of course is better still and transforms the process of 'getting there' into an integral part of the adventure. Think of Goran Kropp's astonishing 1996 Everest climb, after having cycled there (towing all his equipment) from Sweden, or Pauline Sanderson's journey by bike from the Dead Sea to Everest, which she and her team also then climbed.

Fourth, are there other ways of reducing the carbon footprint of the adventure? Perhaps surprisingly, cycling can actually have a higher carbon footprint than driving, if the cyclist is powered primarily by meat. The environmentalist Jonathon Porritt (2004) has argued that it is better to be a vegetarian in a Hummer than a meat-eater on a bicycle! Can the proportion of meat that fuels the adventure be reduced? Are there other ways in which you could lower the carbon footprint of your rations? Whatever the kind of food you are using, do you have to take it all with you or can you buy at least some of it locally? Where has it been produced? Could you buy more local beer and less of the imported stuff?

Fifth is equipment. According to the Worldwatch Institute (Starke and Mastny, 2010, p. 4), 'the average European uses 43 kilograms of resources daily, and the average American uses 88 kilograms. All in all, the world extracts the equivalent of 112 Empire State Buildings from the earth every single day.' We buy, use and consume vast amounts of stuff, and it all has an energy cost (see Chapters 4 and 13 for theoretical discussions of the commodification of adventure). Although recycling is becoming more widespread and is definitely an advance on throwing stuff 'away', it is still a process that requires energy. *Reusing* is better. Ellen MacArthur talks about the eye-opening experience of returning to the 'normal world' from the world of long-distance sailing, where you only have what you have. If it breaks, you find a way to fix it. Everything gets mended or reused. This is a huge contrast to life on dry land, where we buy stuff without thinking and may dispose of it just as thoughtlessly. Even better than reusing or repairing is *refusing*: do we need the stuff in the first place? The company Patagonia, for example, long an advocate of making gear that lasts with as low a footprint as possible, makes this point in their striking 'don't buy this jacket' advert. They go beyond recycling to provoke the question: how much stuff do we really need? How much stuff do we really need to adventure?

The sixth stage shifts the focus onto benefits. Once you have reduced the carbon costs as far as possible, could the benefits of your adventure be increased or enhanced? Could you add a positive environmental or social dimension, by engaging with a local conservation project, for example? Could you give talks about your experiences on your return, thus using the adventure as a way of raising awareness about climate change and positive ways of responding to it? You might decide to set yourself the challenge of keeping your adventures within a self-adopted carbon budget and write about the experiences this generated. You might choose not to buy any new kit for a year and keep a blog. You might show leadership by reducing your own carbon footprint in all sorts of ways that will inspire others to follow suit.

Seventh, and finally, once you've worked through the process of maximizing the positive impacts of your adventure and minimizing its negative ones, the best thing that you can do is go for a bit longer and make the most of it. Celebrate that adventure to the full!

The climate change context means that both the costs and the benefits of any given adventure really need to come under the spotlight. This doesn't have to be negative, however. Microadventures can be cheaper and more frequent. The challenge of adventuring within self-imposed carbon limits can foster creativity. Furthermore, 'carbon budgets' can lead you to spend more time in closer places that are every bit as wonderful as those on the other side of the planet. Having imposed a 'no more than once every three years' flying ration on myself, I have spent much more time sea-kayaking in Scotland. Whereas I used to hanker after new places, I now doubt I could find more wonderful islands for kayaking than the Hebrides anywhere in the world. The more I paddle there, the more I want to return.

Multiple-planet living: the need for a 'new normal'

Perhaps the biggest win–win, though, is the potential that adventure has to offer a different perspective on our ordinary lives, and the values that underpin them. This in turn opens up the possibility of questioning and changing our lives. This is critically important because climate change is not the only global-level environmental problem we face. And, potentially catastrophic as it is, climate change, at the end of the day, is only a symptom. Modern, Western, industrialized lifestyles – our lifestyles – are utterly unsustainable. If everyone on earth had the lifestyle of an average Western European, by 2050 we would need more than two planet earths (World Wildlife Fund, 2010, 2012). We like to think we are the most intelligent species on the planet, yet we are systematically destroying our own habitat, as report after report makes clear (see, for example, United Nations Environment Programme, 2007, 2012). Our dependence on the ecological systems of which we are a part is not a socially or culturally constructed aspect of our lives; it's an objective reality that we simply cannot change. As Christopher Manes (cited in Jensen, 2004, p. 15) puts it: 'A society can't simply destroy and recreate its ecological foundations as if it were some institution like the local supermarket.'

And it's our ecological foundations that we are now threatening. The film *Age of Stupid* has an explanation for this. We are the generation that knew about climate change and could have chosen to tackle it – but didn't. We are the age of stupid. Erik Assadourian (2010) has another explanation, and one that is arguably both more convincing and more constructive. According to Assadourian, we are not stupid, just normal. 'Multiple-planet' lives are lived by ordinary people. None of us wakes up in the morning intent on trashing the planet, yet our lives are lived in such a way that this becomes the cumulative result. We use vast amounts of energy and we buy, use and discard vast amounts of stuff. An astonishing quantity of this stuff is based on oil – everything from plastic to pharmaceuticals. Of course, all commercial products take energy to produce, package, transport, market, sell and dispose of. Industrialized lifestyles – the lifestyles of almost everyone reading this book – are powered by 100,000 years of ancient sunlight every year, and rising. In 2011, despite everything we know about climate change, our global carbon emissions not only went up when they urgently needed to be falling; they went up by a record amount (International Energy Agency, 2011).

There are explanations for this rise that relate to our growth-based economic systems, but this discussion is beyond the scope of this chapter. A key point, however, is that our economies need people to buy more and more consumer goods. This, environmentalists and some economists argue, is supported by a set of social norms and values that tell us we need certain kinds of material goods to be happy, that our status and identity are tied up with these things, and that our success and quality of life can be defined in increasingly materialistic terms.

Philosophers like Peter Singer (1991) argue that we need systematically to question our own beliefs, values and assumptions – the assumptions of our age. Sociologists make a similar point with different language, when they discuss the way individual behaviour is 'normalized' by social norms and values. Bourdieu, as we have seen in Chapter 8, believes that 'human beings have a degree of conscious control (agency) over their lives, the ability to step beyond the "norm", and challenge or reject the dominant doxa (cultural beliefs)' (see p. 80 in this book). It follows from the arguments in this current chapter that we have a profound and urgent need to do exactly this – to examine the social norms, values and beliefs that support our high-carbon ways of life and which make them seem both normal and desirable, despite their fantastically destructive environmental (and social) consequences.

Adventure and the 'new normal'

Adventures can reproduce our mainstream, carbon-era values, beliefs and norms. They can be based on high levels of energy consumption without being questioned. They can involve huge amounts of specialized equipment and clothing, and fall into the status-driven obsession not just with stuff but with the right kind of stuff – with this year's best models. Adventures can buy into consumerist indicators of a high quality of life, and they can reproduce industrialized society's tendency to value the outdoor environment in a purely instrumental way: as the place where we get our resources, or as the arena in which we play, push ourselves, compete or even conquer.

Adventures, however, also have the potential to be much more radical. They can offer us different perspectives from the ones to which we are accustomed, and give us opportunities to step out of our normal cultural field. Adventures can create the opportunity to see things differently and to question our own habitus (see Chapter 8). How much stuff do we really need? Is it really acceptable to fly halfway around the world for a physical challenge, if runaway climate change will be the cumulative consequence of all these flights? Is quality of life really about quantity of stuff or could it be understood in terms of quality of relationships, quality of community and quality of time? Is it appropriate to see the 'outdoor environment' as just an arena for our personal development or as an outdoor gym – or should we spend time getting to know its other inhabitants, too? If we asked these questions, we might return like Ellen MacArthur, who was suddenly able to see how much energy and stuff we use and waste, and the values and norms that sustain this. If she was shocked by what she saw, and felt empowered to find a different way, so too might other adventurers be. Of course, it is almost a cliché that adventurers may value time and freedom to explore more highly than money and status; that the ambition of working nine to five to earn money to buy stuff we don't really need can seem suddenly absurd; and that consumerist values in general can look shallow, illusory or even irrelevant from a mountainside or ocean-wave perspective. We all need a basic level of material wealth but, beyond a certain point, there is compelling evidence that more money and possessions do not lead to more happiness. Adventures can offer life-changing glimpses of different and less materialistic, but potentially more meaningful, ways of living.

Conclusions

Our species is at a critical juncture. Will we take the chance to create a 'carbon-light' era while we still have it? Or will we bring catastrophic climate change upon ourselves? We need leadership, which the outdoor field could offer. It has the advantage of starting with a higher than average degree of connection to the outdoor environment that climate change and other environmental problems are impacting so severely upon. It is good at connecting actions with consequences, and it has great potential for opening debate and inspiring pro-environmental attitudes and actions. Adventures can offer unique opportunities to critique the values, assumptions and norms that sustain high-carbon normality, while showing us examples of how things could be different. Alternatively, we could remain (temporarily) with a relatively uncontested model of high-carbon adventure exploration that, in the end, will literally cost us the earth. We all need a new normal – new ways of living that are low carbon, high quality and completely unexceptional. Our challenge is to move fast in that direction and create high-quality lives that don't cost the earth. Adventures can be part of these high-quality, low-impact lives. Win-win.

Further reading

Inspiring accounts of expedition adventures can be found in:

Crane, R. and Crane, N. (1985) *Bicycles up Kilimanjaro*, Somerset: Oxford Illustrated Press.
Kropp, G. (1999) *Ultimate high*, New York: Random House.
MacArthur, E. (2010) *Full circle*, London: Penguin.
Sanderson, P. (2011) *The world's longest climb*, Derbyshire: Grafika.
Thesiger, W. (1979) *Desert, marsh and mountain: The world of a nomad*, London: Collins.

For more on adventure, cycling and the debate about how profound the changes we need to make to tackle climate change really are, see:

Rawles, K. (2012) *The Carbon Cycle: Crossing the Great Divide*, Uig, Lewis: Two Ravens Press.

For a thorough and readable overview of climate change (solutions as well as problems), try:

Gore, A. (2009) *Our Choice: A Plan to Solve the Climate Crisis*, London: Bloomsbury.

For a thought-provoking critique of consumerism, Assadourian's article (referenced below) is a great place to start. Much of the rest of *State of the World 2010* is also worth reading.

References

Assadourian, E. (2010) 'The rise and fall of consumer cultures', in L. Starke and L. Mastny (eds), *State of the world 2010: Transforming cultures from consumerism to sustainability. A Worldwatch Institute report on progress towards a sustainable society* (pp. 3–20), London: Earthscan.

Berners-Lee, M. (2010) *How bad are bananas? The carbon footprint of everything*, London: Profile Books.

Humphreys, A. (2012) 'Year of microadventure'. Online, available at: http://www.alastair humphreys.com/adventures/year-microadventure/ (accessed 2 October 2012).

International Energy Agency (2011) Reported in the *Guardian*, 29 May.

IPCC (2007) *2007 Report* (vols 1–4), Intergovernmental Panel on Climate Change. Online, available at: http://www.ipcc.ch/, summary available at: http://www.ipcc.ch/ publications_and_data/ar4/syr/en/spm.html (accessed 2 October 2012).

Jensen, D. (2004) *Listening to the land: Conversations about nature, culture and eros*, Whiteriver Junction, VT: Chelsea Green.

Miles, J.C. and Priest, S. (1990) *Adventure education*, State College, PA: Venture.

Monbiot, G. (2006) *Heat: How to stop the planet burning*, London: Allen Lane.

Pike, C.J. and Beames, S.K. (2007) 'A critical interactionist analysis of "youth development" expeditions', *Leisure Studies*, 26(2), 147–59.

Porritt, J. (2004) Talk given at launch of Compassion in World Farming's 'Eat Less Meat' campaign, London.

Singer, P. (1991) *Animal liberation*, London: Thorsons.

Starke, L. and Mastny, L. (eds) (2010) *State of the world 2010: Transforming cultures from consumerism to sustainability. A Worldwatch Institute report on progress towards a sustainable society*. London: Earthscan.

United Nations Environment Programme (2007) 'GEO4 environment for development'. Online, available at: http://www.unep.org/geo/geo4.asp (accessed 2 October 2012).

United Nations Environment Programme (2012) 'GEO5 environment for the future we want'. Online, available at: http://www.unep.org/geo/pdfs/geo5/GEO5_report_full_ en.pdf (accessed 2 October 2012).

Whitty, J. (2007) 'Animal extinction – the greatest threat to mankind', *Independent*, 30 April. Online, available at: http://www.independent.co.uk/environment/animal-extinction— the-greatest-threat-to-mankind-397939.html (accessed 2 October 2012).

Wilson, B. (2008) *Blazing paddles: A Scottish coastal odyssey*, Uig, Lewis: Two Ravens Press.

World Bank Group (2012) 'CO$_2$ emissions (metric tons per capita)'. Online, available at: http://data.worldbank.org/indicator/EN.ATM.CO2E.PC (accessed 29 September 2012).

World Wildlife Fund (2010, 2012) 'Living planet report'. Online, available at: http://wwf. panda.org/about_our_earth/all_publications/living_planet_report/ (accessed 2 October 2012).

15

CONCLUSIONS ON OUTDOOR ADVENTURE AND SOCIAL THEORY

Elizabeth C.J. Pike and Simon Beames

In the introduction to this book, we indicated that we would not cover every single social theory or discuss every issue that is pertinent to understanding the social world of outdoor adventure. Other editors also may have organized this book differently. We have attempted, through this series of essays, to illustrate how social theory may help us to better understand outdoor adventure, and have drawn on the theories and the scholars whom we believed were best placed to illuminate these issues.

We have learned that social theory offers a way of describing, analysing and understanding outdoor adventure. We now know that we can use this knowledge to make sense of these activities and the experiences of people who take part in them, because social theories help us to ask questions that we may not have otherwise considered. In the course of this book we have learned that many people believe that outdoor adventure offers meaningful, educational, life-changing activity. On the other hand, we have also learned that outdoor adventure can contribute to social problems. As a result, our beliefs about engaging in adventurous activities in the outdoors are less simple, and more complex and 'messy', than we might have previously believed. Furthermore, we have learned that we do not always have sufficient evidence to support the claims that we might make about these activities. In order to make sense of the role of outdoor adventure in people's lives, we need to collate more evidence about what is actually going on in the world of outdoor adventure, and why certain activities are organized and performed in particular ways. We can draw on social theory to help us analyse and understand this information, and then use this knowledge to consider how outdoor adventure might be changed and improved.

The authors of the chapters presented in this book have drawn on several theoretical frameworks as a means of raising key questions about outdoor adventure. We will not repeat all of these here but instead identify some of the themes that have recurred throughout the book. These are: the relationship of structure and agency; how historical trends can inform our understanding of contemporary practice; the influence of capitalism and global economics on outdoor adventure; and social inequalities. Let us consider each of these in turn.

The relationship of structure and agency

Some social theories (interactionism, post-structuralism and some feminist theories) tend to focus on agency, or the ways in which people are believed to act freely and make their own rational choices about their lifestyles and behaviour. Other theories (functionalism, Marxism and some figurational sociology) favour structure as a means of understanding human behaviour, by suggesting that our choices are controlled by social structures such as the economy, law and education. For example, in Chapter 3, Brown draws on the work of Durkheim to explain how outdoor adventure may serve as a way of inculcating in us social norms and values that then influence individual behaviour. These norms and values may range from learning to obey instructions and supporting team-mates to wearing particular designer kit. Similarly, Zink's review of the work of Foucault (Chapter 10) helps us to consider the relationships of individuals and broader structures that create environments in which activities become meaningful.

In each chapter, the authors have highlighted a need to understand outdoor adventure through considering structure and agency, while recognizing the weaknesses in both paradigms. In Chapter 8, Beames and Telford draw on the work of Bourdieu to examine the experiences of two fictional climbers, who are exposed to different climbing cultures that influence their own lifestyle choices and behaviour. While they have autonomy, or agency, to make these choices, they are also affected by the social structures to which they have been exposed throughout their lives.

In order to fully understand outdoor adventure, we need to learn more of the activities themselves, how they evolved, the various ways in which people experience them, and the underlying factors that control and facilitate them. In order to understand outdoor adventure in contemporary societies, it is helpful to take a historical perspective in order to learn about the lives of the people who created and developed these activities, and the influence of power, money and other resources on the ways in which these activities have progressed over the years.

Historical trends

When we consider the history of outdoor adventure, it is important to recognize that there is never 'one history' of any event. There will always be different histories, as people who experience events will have their own interpretation and lived experiences of what happened. Furthermore, there is rarely a blueprint for how activities are going to progress in different historical periods; changes happen as a result of actions taken by different people at various times. We can understand these developments by drawing on social theories to ask key questions and reflect on the main trends. For example, in Chapter 14, Rawles comments on some of the unintended consequences of outdoor adventure which have ironically damaged the very environment that participants enjoy while doing their activities. Rawles shows us how social theory helps us to question some of our actions, and suggests ways in which we might transform future practice in order to protect the very planet that enables our outdoor adventurous activities.

In Beedie's contribution (Chapter 9), we are introduced to the work of Giddens, who also considered the relationship between individuals and institutions, or structure and agency. He argues that outdoor adventure practices have been influenced by participation trends and practice over time. For example, the risks we learn to take and the equipment we are trained to use in outdoor adventurous activities become routine and are eventually established as 'rules' of conduct that subsequently control how we behave in specific environments. These are not formal laws but nevertheless become understood as desirable ways to experience outdoor adventure during this particular historical period, and within certain societies and social groups.

Atkinson's chapter on Parkour (Chapter 6) challenges us to consider participants in outdoor adventurous activities as historically developing networks of actors. In other words, these activities and their participants have not appeared out of thin air; their engagement has emerged over time and in particular geographical places through interactions with other people.

Each of the activities discussed in this book has been modified and developed during different historical periods, as people have adapted them to suit their own needs and broader social changes. Arguably, some of the most significant influences on the development of outdoor adventurous activities in modern societies in recent years have been economic factors, and these were discussed in several chapters as highlighted in the next section.

The influence of capitalism and global economics

Varley and Loynes (Chapters 4 and 13) develop the historical and economic analysis of outdoor adventure by introducing us to the concepts of rationalization, globalization and McDonaldization. These explain how outdoor adventurous activities have become systematically organized over time in order to demonstrate how they offer benefits to participants. The benefits are not only related to the intrinsic worth or pleasure in the activity, but also influenced by the extrinsic value or how much money can be made from the activity. Consequently, our activities become controlled and predictable in order to guarantee a particular experience.

As Tracey explains in Chapter 5, the work of Gramsci helps us to analyse the ways in which these new forms of established activities are carefully marketed by those who can make money from them, and how participants gradually adopt these forms of outdoor adventure. So, we learn that we can buy membership of clubs, purchase artificially constructed indoor 'outdoor' adventure or safe tourist 'adventure', and pay for coaching qualifications that then enable us to earn a salary as a coach. In Chapter 2, Cater and Dash draw on a Marxist perspective to argue that we become alienated from the authentic experience as we seek the instant gratification of a thrill rather than building the skills and knowledge needed to participate independently in the activity. Social theory helps us to understand how these changes have altered the ways in which many of us now experience outdoor adventure, and raises questions about the ways in which we may wish to develop and participate in these activities in the future.

Social inequalities

Many of us who participate and work in outdoor adventure would like to think that it offers an alternative to traditional sporting activities, not least by being inclusive of all who wish to participate regardless of gender, age, ethnicity or disability. We have learned in this book that social inequalities still exist in many areas of outdoor adventure, and that more work needs to be done to make these activities more inclusive.

Beedie and Loynes (Chapters 9 and 13) both refer to the classed nature of numerous outdoor adventurous activities that have excluded many from lower social classes, while privileging those who already have significant economic and social capital. Similarly, in Chapter 12 Pike and Weinstock consider the ways in which those perceived to have 'frail' bodies, whether through age or disability, may be discouraged from participation in outdoor adventure despite the benefits experienced by those who are able to take part. Allin and West (Chapter 11) have explained how feminist theories help us to understand the discriminatory practices that mean many women and girls are still not offered the same opportunities to experience outdoor adventurous activities as men and boys and, as a result, do not enter leadership positions to the same extent as their male peers. They draw on a variety of different feminist theories to question whether women need help to reach the same level as their male counterparts or whether the basis of outdoor adventure itself needs challenging.

The adventure starts here!

It was the intention of this book to serve as a starting point for your journey into the critical analysis of outdoor adventure. In the opening chapter, we defined adventure as a challenge with an uncertain outcome and inescapable consequences. We hope that, from here, you will rise to the challenge, and that on your journey you will continue to study in more depth the theories and themes that have been presented, to consider other theories and to do your own research into outdoor adventure informed and inspired by social theory. The outcome will be uncertain, but the consequences for yourselves and the people with whom you engage in outdoor adventure could be incredibly positive. Ultimately, we encourage you to use what you have learned to harness the power of outdoor adventure in order to contribute to social change and make the world a safer, more humane and better place. Now that's an adventure!

INDEX